RTI
With Differentiated
Instruction, Grades K–5

RTI

With Differentiated Instruction, Grades K–5

A Classroom Teacher's Guide

Jodi O'Meara

CORWIN
A SAGE Company

CORWIN
A SAGE Company

FOR INFORMATION:

Corwin
A SAGE Company
2455 Teller Road
Thousand Oaks, California 91320
(800) 233-9936
Fax: (800) 417-2466
www.corwin.com

SAGE Ltd.
1 Oliver's Yard
55 City Road
London EC1Y 1SP
United Kingdom

SAGE India Pvt. Ltd.
B 1/I 1 Mohan Cooperative
Industrial Area
Mathura Road, New Delhi 110 044
India

SAGE Asia-Pacific Pte. Ltd.
33 Pekin Street #02-01
Far East Square
Singapore 048763

Acquisitions Editor: Hudson Perigo
Associate Editor: Allison Scott
Editorial Assistant: Lisa Whitney
Production Editor: Cassandra Margaret Seibel
Copy Editor: Sarah J. Duffy
Typesetter: C&M Digitals (P) Ltd.
Proofreader: Susan Schon
Indexer: Wendy Allex
Cover Designer: Michael Dubowe
Permissions Editor: Adele Hutchinson

Printed in the United States of America.

Library of Congress Cataloging-in-Publication Data

O'Meara, Jodi.
RTI with differentiated instruction, grades K-5: a classroom teacher's guide / Jodi O'Meara.

p. cm.
Includes bibliographical references and index.

ISBN 978-1-4129-9527-6 (pbk.)

1. Remedial teaching—United States. 2. Response to intervention (Learning disabled children). 3. Slow learning children—Education—United States. 4. Learning disabled children—Education—United States. 5. Reading (Elementary)—United States. I. Title.

LB1029.R4O635 2011 371.9—dc22 2011000470

This book is printed on acid-free paper.

11 12 13 14 15 10 9 8 7 6 5 4 3 2 1

Contents

Acknowledgments

My most humble and sincere thank you goes out to the team at Corwin and especially Hudson Perigo, whom I admire with awe and inspiration. I have such respect and trust for your judgment, and you have continued to recognize and polish the gems you see in my work. I have become a better person and professional in your hands. I am honored to know you and treasure you as a professional and friend. Great appreciation also goes out to the Corwin team who has worked hard to create such a wonderful resource; thank you, Allison, Lisa, Cassandra, and Sarah.

I also want to express the deep gratitude and respect I have for my mother, who again helped me with this project. You have always amazed me with your success in life and as a mother. You have been there with guidance and support for my whole life as a lighthouse to show me the right direction and as a rock of stability and safety. Thanks for being there for me and cheering me on so that I had the confidence to take on these projects and grow. It is so cool to see someone I admire so much beam with such pride! Thank you for your strength, wisdom, guidance, and unconditional love and support as a mom and best friend.

I need to also thank my other "mom," Janie Bartels, who has been my Florida mom for more than 10 years. You have also been there for me with unconditional support and friendship. You have encouraged me and cheered me on as well as helped me in countless ways on a daily basis. I could not make it through a week without you!

Thank you to Patrick Ewin for your personal tutoring to help me with the accuracy of this book. I appreciate your expertise as a statistician and, even more, your friendship.

Thank you to my dear friend Dr. Shelby Robertson. Your friendship and knowledge has been invaluable to me. Thank you for lending me a shoulder to stress on, an ear to bend, and a critical eye to improve. Thank you for your expertise and help and most of all for your friendship, shopping dates, Aidan anecdotes, and smiles.

Another huge thank you to my special friend and partner from the Florida Inclusion Network, Mike Muldoon. You have been a great friend and professional development partner for some time now. I am so fortunate to work and grow with you. Thanks for your support on this project and all my endeavors.

On a personal note, thank you to grandpa and grandma, Fred and Ruth Choate. You are amazing people and the foundation of a big, wonderful family. I am so pleased to make you proud of me. Thank you to Jeff, Michelle, Emily, and Jennifer Choate. Thanks to Jon, Susanne, Aidan, and Elijah Choate. Family is always my happy place, my motivation for everything I do, and the most meaningful part of my life. You are each a part of me and everything I do.

Thank you to Russell Schall for your love, support, and encouragement. It is great to see how proud you are of me. You make me feel very special.

Finally, I can't go without saying thank you to so many educators in Manatee County who have left me speechless and moved by the amount of support and friendship you have shown with *Beyond Differentiated Instruction* and this book. I have been so touched by the support and shared happiness for my accomplishments. So much of what I learned in order to write this book has been spurred through questions and learning, side by side, with so many of you. We have grown as professionals together—teachers, paraprofessionals, school administrators, district leaders, parents, and students themselves. It has been so much more special to share it with so many friends and the community of which I am a part.

PUBLISHER'S ACKNOWLEDGMENTS

Corwin gratefully acknowledges the contributions of the following reviewers:

Ronda Gregg
Director of Special Services
Litchfield, NH

Angela Becton, NBCT
Gifted Program Specialist
National Board Support
Johnston County Schools
Smithfield, NC

David Tudor
Program Supervisor, Learning
   Improvement
Office of Superintendent of
   Public Instruction
Portland, OR

Shelly Dostal
Director, K–6 Principal and
   Curriculum
Raymond Central Public
   Schools
Valparaiso, NE

Shelby Robertson
Associate Director of
   Mathematics
RTI Teaching Learning
   Connections
University of
   Central Florida
Orlando, FL

About the Author

 **Jodi O'Meara** is an independent educational consultant of Jodi O'Meara, Inc. She also serves in Manatee County, Florida, as a curriculum specialist for students with special needs. Jodi provides professional development for educators and administrators at local, state, national, and international conferences and workshops. With over 15 years as a teacher and administrator of general education, special education, and gifted education, she recognizes the diverse needs of students and teachers. Her own experiences with differentiated instruction were first evident in the multiple stories of her own teaching in *Chicken Soup for the Teacher's Soul* (2002). More recently, Jodi's work includes *Beyond Differentiated Instruction* (2010) and *RTI With Differentiated Instruction, Grades 6–8: A Classroom Teacher's Guide* (2011), both published by Corwin.

Jodi specializes in the areas of differentiated instruction for both students with special needs and students identified as gifted. She is a former president of the Florida Association for Gifted and is on the Board of Directors for the Family Network on Disabilities in her local area. She has been involved with writing state curriculum for students in general education, in gifted education, and those identified as having significant disabilities.

Jodi is a strong advocate for both teachers and students. She believes that teachers hold the keys to our future and that today's students have amazing and unlimited potential. She believes that with changes to the educational system allowing educators to honor different strengths and needs, it is possible to foster every student in reaching his or her highest potential. She is committed to supporting teachers in making that difference. Jodi can be reached at jodi@jodiomeara.com.

Introduction

The year is 1979. A third-grade teacher requests a meeting with parents of one of her students one day in October. The teacher is concerned about Kathryn. It seems Kathryn is not keeping up with the other students in third grade. Kathryn struggles with both her reading and her math. She is in the lowest reading group. The teacher keeps Kathryn in from recess for two days a week to provide her with extra time to work more slowly and more carefully. Kathryn also stays after school for extra help three days a week. The extra help she receives is based on materials that come with the reading textbooks designed to provide additional practice for struggling students. Kathryn's parents meet with the teacher and are asked to help Kathryn with her math facts using flash cards.

The teacher in this scenario was working to meet Kathryn's needs. She was using strategies and materials that she had available to her, which included the parents in supporting Kathryn's learning. Some of those elements still exist in our classrooms today. Over time, educators have addressed concerns about students with their parents. Teachers have always worked to help struggling learners. However, we have learned to approach these situations differently. Now we extend our reach to resources that exist beyond the classroom and the textbook. We collaborate with multiple professionals to consider nontraditional options. Most important, we use data to make instructional decisions and use what we know from research to select approaches to assist students.

The year is now 2011. A third-grade teacher requests a meeting to discuss Rebecca, a student about whom she has concerns. She invites a fourth-grade teacher, a teacher of gifted students, an administrator, a guidance counselor, the parents, and the teacher this student had in second grade. At this meeting she expresses concerns about her ability to challenge Rebecca. Rebecca is very bright and already knows content far beyond the third-grade curricular standards. The teacher reflects this by sharing results from Rebecca's universal screening measures along with the benchmark assessment data and standardized testing results from the past. She asks the second-grade teacher for suggestions of how to meet Rebecca's need for more challenge based on what the

1

teacher did for Rebecca last year. She asks the teacher of gifted students and the fourth-grade teacher for suggestions or options to provide more challenge. The administrator suggests that Rebecca attend reading in the fourth-grade class and that the teacher of gifted students pursue an evaluation and determine how Rebecca could be challenged in a program for gifted and talented students.

In the same class with Rebecca is Jerry. Jerry has been struggling in reading for the past few years. His DIBELS scores, benchmark assessments scores, and standardized results all put him in the bottom quartile for reading performance. Again, the third-grade teacher calls a meeting with some key stakeholders, including Jerry's parents. The teacher is already working with Jerry before school three days a week, and he is getting additional reading instruction that is specific to the areas of weakness as shown by his assessments. Jerry's parents are working with him at home using a research-based software program. The reading specialist suggests she work with Jerry for 30 minutes two times a week. She will implement some specialized approaches after completing a diagnostic assessment. The third-grade teacher and she will both collect data to see whether there is evidence of any improvement over the next five weeks of this trial.

Good teaching is and has always been good teaching. A teacher who cares and does what it takes to meet the needs of each student as an individual will always be a good teacher. These elements have been the same for as long as our educational system has existed. However, educational policies, practices, and processes have changed over time, and research has focused on creating more systematic approaches to curriculum and instruction. Two components that have evolved into education as we know it today are differentiated instruction (DI) and Response to Intervention/Instruction (RTI). Together, they ensure that there are no students who fall through the cracks and whose education needs are overlooked.

DI and RTI aim to meet the needs of all learners. They are supports for each other, with a common goal. They are not parallel initiatives on separate tracks but more of a marriage, where one and one become more than two. They are two separate frameworks and practices while being meshed and woven together. In some ways they look the same in a classroom; however, each brings certain characteristics that strengthen the other. Most important, both have the same intent—to provide and foster a system in which students are challenged and supported in reaching their highest potential as students and lifelong learners.

This book is intended to examine these two topics and their relationship to each other from the eyes of the classroom teacher. There are vast implications for these initiatives, many of which fall onto the shoulders of the classroom teacher. This book provides the classroom teacher with direct, clear, and practical strategies and systems to help the teacher simultaneously implement DI and RTI in a practical "how-to" format. It examines the two frameworks and practices in relationship to all learners—with and without labels. It includes those in general education, those in English language learner programs, those in special education programs, and even those in gifted programs.

Part I of this book begins by clarifying the definitions and implementation practices involved with both DI and RTI. After establishing a clear definition of RTI, Chapter 1 presents the definitions and practices related to the approach. It also addresses the critical principles of RTI and then addresses some implications of the possible changes in practices that may result from the research. Then, Chapter 2 examines DI, along with the 10-step process of differentiation. In Chapter 3, RTI and DI are merged together to examine commonalities and differences.

Part II is dedicated to Tier 1 of the RTI model. Because this tier impacts all teachers, it receives the most attention. Tier 1 represents the core instruction that is provided by the classroom teacher. This is the stage at which DI first takes place. Chapters 4–6 look at what happens in the classroom with regard to instruction, assessment, and the environment. Each of those components contains elements of both RTI and DI; they are intertwined throughout. This part of the book examines what goes on in the classroom to effectively implement both practices. Since the framework of RTI is more definitive, it is the structure used as the skeleton for discussing both, although each is as important as the other.

In Part III, Tiers 2 and 3 are addressed through the eyes of the classroom teacher. Therefore, the chapters in this section are not about how to establish a schoolwide system for providing the supports and services at these tiers. Instead, these chapters address how a teacher within a classroom can best provide services and collaborate with others to recruit supports and services at Tiers 2 and 3. The tiers are not addressed in terms of systems and processes, but instead in terms of practices and implications. Strategies and methods of curriculum, instruction, and environmental supports as well as accommodations are all considered. Practices of data collection and methods of determining the data to collect are addressed. The emphasis is on what to do to support students within the system and how to implement differentiation and interventions rather than the systems themselves. Finally, the problem-solving team is addressed again through the eyes of a classroom teacher. This includes what to expect and how to prepare information to share with the team.

The book is designed to bring research and theory to life in the classroom. RTI and DI are not about completing forms or lesson plans. They are practices that may involve those actions, but they are done as a means to an end rather than the end in itself. Examples and practical suggestions are provided to illustrate and support implementation. The forms included are suggested aspects to be considered as school districts create their own personalized forms and protocols.

Each chapter concludes with questions to consider. These are designed for both self-reflection and professional discussion. They provide a venue for further investigation or consideration. They are not intended to be a quiz, but rather a means of encouraging deeper conversations at the application level. The intent is to guide possible next steps to move forward and grow professionally. After all, that is the intent of the entire work!

I hope you enjoy this journey through this exploration of RTI and DI. As a teacher, you will be able to see glimpses of your classroom in the examples and ideas. You will see how your efforts to meet the many needs of students are aligned to these larger frameworks. You will gain insights regarding your classroom and your practices. You may discover answers to old questions and develop brand-new questions as well. And you will receive affirmation that good teaching practices that discerningly meet the needs of students as individuals will continue to be the best teaching practices.

PART I

RTI, Differentiated Instruction, and Their Marriage

The Foundation

1

Principles of RTI and Implications in the Classroom

Students come to us at all levels from all different backgrounds, experiences, and abilities. We cannot ignore these differences and assume all students are ready for page 1 on the first day of school. We also cannot deny that others come to us thirsty for the information on page 250 on that same day. Despite these differences, the same instrument will measure all these students on a given day. They will all compete for jobs in the same workplace on a given day as well. Teaching is an amazing challenge!

WHAT IS RTI?

While RTI is currently one of the most talked-about initiatives in education, it remains one of the greatest mysteries with the most unanswered questions. Presently, there are still debates as to the RTI acronym itself. Some literature calls it "Response to Intervention," other documents call it "Response to Instruction," and still others call it "Response to Intervention and Instruction." In practice, RTI is both a focus on the student's response to instruction as well as the student's response to intervention. The term *response* also refers to the teacher's response to student performance and data as well.

The more the concepts of RTI are explored, the more meaning each of the words holds. Some systems have even moved away from the name RTI to call it other names such as Multi-Tiered Support Systems. Whatever you call it, this multifaceted educational initiative has stirred questions from just about every aspect of the educational system. What are the implications for special education or gifted education? What are the responsibilities of the general education classroom teacher? How does an administrator establish an RTI team within a school? In what ways does RTI change the roles of the support team players such as guidance counselors, psychologists, and social workers? There seem to be as many questions as confirmations.

One reason for the large number of unanswered questions is that this initiative touches on so many aspects of the educational system. Since the mid 1990s, standards-based reform efforts and student accountability efforts have been center stage and influencing the focus of educational change (Rudebusch, 2008). In 2001, with the passage of the No Child Left Behind (NCLB) law, the focus shifted from providing services to monitoring the quality and effectiveness of those services. In addition, with the 2004 reauthorization of the Individuals with Disabilities Education Act (IDEA), now known as the Individuals with Disabilities Education Improvement Act (IDEIA), the efforts for all students to have access to researched-based high-quality curriculum was even more greatly reinforced (Rudebusch, 2008). Greater demands of Adequate Yearly Progress (AYP) for all students as well as for each subgroup defined by the NCLB law continue to increase the pressure for accountability based on assessment data and highest student achievement for all students. All of these forces have broadened the scope of personnel involved with these efforts and implementation of RTI, which encompasses both accountability and highest student achievement for all learners. RTI has been supported by a number of major initiatives, including the National Reading Panel, the National Research Council Panel on Minority Overrepresentation, and the President's Committee on Excellence in Special Education, to name a few (National Association of State Directors of Special Education [NASDSE], 2006). Therefore, there is not a single stakeholder within the educational system who remains untouched by the efforts of RTI. Consensus reports from multiple national panels, along with technical assistance papers and white papers from national educational organizations, show evidence of RTI's all-inclusive nature.

So while educators are working to keep up with the research and professional learning about RTI, each is also asking, "How does this affect me?" And the answer is . . . in every way. RTI is a change in thinking about how the educational system functions to meet the needs of students. RTI happens all day, every day for all students rather than just during a specific period of time or for a specific group of students (Howard, 2009). It is an integrated system designed to meet the needs of all students by providing them with the supports they need when they need them rather than based on a schedule or calendar. RTI approaches the challenges a learner faces by proactively asking, "What can be done to help?" rather than "What can we name this problem?" RTI is a model of prevention rather than failure (NASDSE, 2006). It brings together all the strongest initiatives within education and reflects foundations of NCLB, IDEIA, differentiated instruction, positive behavioral support, inclusion, and teacher collaboration efforts.

While RTI is supported and influenced by several special education movements, it is not a new venue to identify students for special education. It is also not a framework of forms and procedures to formalize meetings and eligibility processes. RTI involves all students, including those who are high-achieving and gifted. It is founded on instruction and student achievement and begins in the classroom. RTI is for every student who *ever* says, "I don't understand," "I missed it," or even "This is too easy."

With its far-reaching influences, RTI provides a catalyst to move the educational system forward to a point where it has never been before. It demands both philosophical changes as well as changes in practice. It requires all those members of the educational system to look differently at the entire process of teaching, learning, and meeting the needs of students in a variety of ways. It moves differentiated instruction to a whole new plane and changes the way we identify students' needs and serve those students. RTI brings us to an exciting new arena in education and holds new promises for a future educational system that really begins with students at the center.

So what is RTI? There is a great deal of information about it and yet there is still not a consistent answer to that question. There are multiple definitions of RTI. The National Center on Response to Intervention (n.d.-b) defines it as the integration of "assessment and intervention within a multi-level prevention system to maximize student achievement and to reduce behavior problems" (para. 1). RTI includes the practices of identifying students at risk, monitoring student progress, implementing evidence-based interventions, and adjusting the intensity and nature of those interventions based on student performance as reflected in the data.

PRINCIPLES OF RTI

There are consistencies in the characteristics of all RTI efforts. These characteristics have become more important than what names we assign the initials of RTI. The following characteristics describe the essence of this initiative, and it is through these common descriptions that both a philosophy and practice can be developed:

- addresses both academic and behavioral domains
- creates a systematic dynamic process for instruction and intervention
- applies to students in general education, special education, English language, and gifted programs

- demands that all students have access to quality core instruction
- examines student performance, classroom conditions, instructional factors, and schoolwide structures
- expects that some students will need additional supports and services beyond the core curriculum and general behavioral expectations
- provides a process for decision making based on clear data for every student
- requires continuous progress monitoring and formative assessments to drive instruction
- responds to learner needs when they are recognized and involves intervention that comes without a label
- strives to go beyond students making some gains to students making accelerated gains at a rate that will allow them to not fall further behind
- includes aspects beyond the instructional time and considers the student as a whole child

CLASSROOM IMPLICATIONS

RTI addresses both academic and behavioral domains.

Unlike traditional models in education, RTI recognizes the fact that behavior and academics are both equally related to student performance and academic success. Therefore, an RTI model considers the academic well-being of students as well as their behavioral aspects. It acknowledges that learning takes place when learners are in a state that includes both positive cognitive and behavioral conditions. This acknowledges that the best teaching can fall on deaf ears and nonresponsive learners if the learning state is not healthy. In a classroom where students are feeling unsafe or unsure of acceptance or rejection, there is greater likelihood that they will disconnect from learning (Gregory & Kuzmich, 2004). It also acknowledges that in order for students to be successful, structures must be in place for both learning and behavioral expectations.

The implications for the classroom teacher are philosophical and practical in nature. First, students are more than receptacles of knowledge. Expectations must be clear and specific for students to achieve success. These expectations take into account the whole child and go beyond simply the learning expectations. Second, for students to be successful, both academic and behavioral expectations must be clearly stated and addressed. It cannot be assumed that students know the appropriate behaviors and rules of the class culture any more than it can be assumed that they come with the background knowledge needed to process new content. Instructional practices and behavioral and instructional expectations with structures are needed for effective learning to occur.

**RTI creates a systematic dynamic
process for instruction and intervention.**

As a natural by-product, RTI provides a decision-making process based on student data. Assessment is a cornerstone of the model. Multiple levels of assessment are used to make decisions at different levels. Information from screening assessments, diagnostic assessments, and clinical assessments all have a place within the RTI system, and their place is defined. Each of these components works together to provide a framework that is systematic and streamlined in nature.

The tiers of RTI provide a structure for this process of determining the level of support that each student needs. The tiers are not indicators of the students themselves but instead are indicators of levels of support needed. Typically, the most widely used models involve three or four tiers (see Figure 1.1). At Tier 1, all students participate in core instruction and universal behavioral systems. The focus at Tier 1 is a core instruction that is high quality, research-based, systematic, and developmentally appropriate. Universal behavioral systems are schoolwide and classroom-wide systems with clearly stated expectations and consequences. These are positively stated and reinforced. Assessments most widely

Figure 1.1   The RTI Triangle for Academics and Behavior

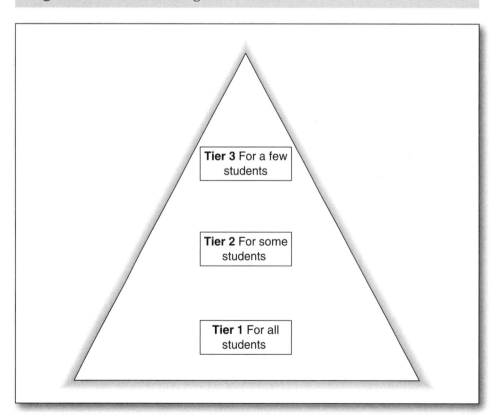

Tier 3 For a few
students

Tier 2 For some
students

Tier 1 For all
students

used in Tier 1 include screening instruments, universal screenings, and progress monitoring tools.

Tier 2 provides more services or supports for students who need something in addition to the core curriculum and instruction or universal behavioral system. This tier is characterized by "something more" and beyond the norm. It includes small-group instruction for reteaching and remediation as well as enrichment for students who need additional challenges. Decisions about when and what to provide for specific students are based on data. These data usually come from more specific diagnostic types of assessments. Decisions about providing more supports or services are made on a case-by-case basis. They are not made just once each year, but rather are constantly adjusted for each learning experience throughout the school year. The objective of providing additional supports at this increased level of intensity is to promote student success in the Tier 1 core curriculum through the use of supplemental services, supports, and materials. The interventions are aligned to the instructional needs determined by assessments during core instruction.

Tier 3 is in place for students who need more than the supplemental supports provided in Tier 2. This tier is characterized by individualized, intensive supports. There are a very small number of students who need this level of intensity of support; however, the expectation is that there will be a few students who need more supports than can be provided even in Tier 2. Data for decision making at this level varies due to the individualized nature of Tier 3. Data collection at this stage may include specialized testing or additional targeted diagnostics. Supports may be provided by someone with specialized skills or expertise in the area of the student's need. The objective of providing additional supports at this increased level of intensity is to promote student success with Tier 2 interventions, which will in turn support the core instruction provided in Tier 1. Tier 3 also directly supports the core instruction through intensive supports and services. The interventions are aligned to the needs evidenced in the small-group instruction of Tier 2 as well as the core instruction in Tier 1. Each tier builds on the one before it, rather than replacing it. A student receiving Tier 3 supports continues to receive core instruction with differentiated supports from Tier 1.

One implication for classroom teachers is the emphasis on, and necessity of, flexible grouping. Teachers must implement flexible grouping practices to respond to learners' needs. This flexible grouping is determined by data rather than by the use of student labels. The purpose is to meet students' needs so that they are able to experience success with the core curriculum. Unlike grouping done for the purpose of community building in the classroom, flexible grouping is intentional and homogeneous in nature. Student performance levels within a group are similar to each other so that students may receive the same instructional supports. Groups are defined by needs rather than by chance or by combining students with wide ranges of ability or because Susie works well with Janie. Students are grouped based on their abilities and needs for instruction.

Groupings change as the content changes. One common example of a flexible grouping practice is guided reading groups.

Another implication here is that the interventions are systematically designed to support what is happening throughout the core instructional experiences. Rather than removing a struggling student and providing interventions in place of the core instruction, these interventions are implemented in addition to and in conjunction with the core instruction. The interventions become systematic and directly connected to the student performance within the core curriculum. The interventions are more likely to be done in an inclusive classroom setting rather than in a separate resource room.

In the past, a struggling student may have been removed for a period of the day to receive additional supports and services. Often these were not connected to the content or skills being learned in the classroom. Services and supports were isolated and disjointed. If a student was struggling in reading, he or she might leave core instruction for reading and go to a resource room. With RTI, the purpose of Tier 2 is to support the student in being successful in Tier 1. The skills keeping the student from experiencing success in Tier 1 are the skills targeted for added supports. These added supports are the Tier 2 services, and they become directly linked to what is happening in Tier 1. Instead of the struggling student missing out on the core instruction, the intervention is delivered at another time in addition to that core instruction. It enhances rather than supplants instruction.

RTI applies to students in general education, special education, English language programs, and gifted programs.

RTI is built on the foundations of powerful legislation such as NCLB and IDEIA. It reinforces the concept that "all means all." RTI does not exclude anyone from this system, which is designed to acknowledge each student as an individual with both strengths and needs. Through data collection, each student is viewed as an individual, in relation to peers and as part of a larger group. The data identify similarities and differences that exist between individual students and groups of students. RTI is rooted in honoring those findings.

RTI is a structural organization for providing supports and services. In the past, unless a student was identified and then qualified as a student with special needs, there was no structure for supports and services. Those students who had an individualized education program (IEP) did have a structure and received services and supports based on needs. In many cases, these supports and services were given outside the regular classroom. RTI creates a system whereby a student may receive systematic supports and services without an IEP. That does not mean that an IEP is no longer necessary. The IEP documents goals within the core curriculum as well as some that may be outside the general education curriculum that a student may need to achieve to experience success. However, because a student has an IEP and qualifies for a program under the Americans with

Disabilities Act, the student still has a need for the RTI structure. The two are simply layered. They do not work as parallel and independent systems, but instead blend into one system. The student will still have needs within the core curriculum at Tier 1, possibly small-group supports at Tier 2 and additionally some individualized supports and services at Tier 3. Even the students with the most significant disabilities need different amounts of supports for different learning tasks. RTI provides the framework to match levels of need to amounts of support.

Because the premise of RTI is to provide systematic supports and services matched to individual needs of students, the model certainly applies to gifted students as well. These students are identified as gifted because they have characteristics that fall outside the general parameters of the educational system's standard expectations. These students have needs that are unique and go beyond the core curriculum. In many instances, students identified as gifted need additional challenge, motivation, behavioral, social, or emotional supports. There are also gifted students who do not excel in all areas and may need supports for a particular area of academic weakness just as students not identified as gifted would. In all of these instances, the students reflect a need that goes beyond the core curriculum at Tier 1.

RTI demands that all students have access to quality core instruction.

The RTI initiative is an interdependent system composed of classroom instruction, student assessment, and problem solving for the purpose of intervention (see Figure 1.2). These three elements come together with each student at the center and rest on a foundation of a quality, research-based, systematic core curriculum.

RTI is aligned to the efforts of IDEIA by emphasizing that all students have access to quality core instruction. This requirement is not new. It has been in place in the educational system since 1997. However, RTI has made it even stronger. Not only is this expectation clearly stated in IDEIA, but RTI takes these efforts a step further by creating some expectations of success within the core instruction. RTI provides

Figure 1.2   Elements of RTI

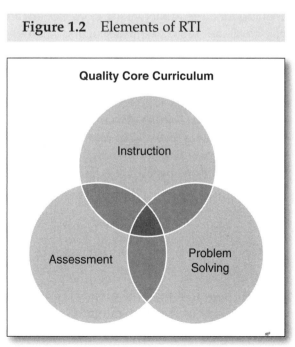

standards that have never been set before in the educational system. RTI is founded on the expectation that all students will receive instruction with a quality, research-based core curriculum and that a substantial number of students will be successful. RTI research historically has set the expectation that approximately 80% of students will be successful when quality instruction has been provided within a strong core curriculum. This same percentage also applies as an expectation of success when a clear universal behavioral program has been implemented.

This is revolutionary for two reasons. The first is that there is now an expectation set forth regarding student success as a whole. The RTI initiative communicates that with high-quality instruction, approximately 80% of students should be successful. Along with that expectation comes the idea that if approximately 80% of students are not successful, it is the system or instruction that needs to change or adjust. This principle clarifies expectations of and for the classroom teacher.

RTI suggests that approximately 80% of students will be successful in learning after quality instruction has been provided. If 80% of students are not successful, it is the instruction that needs to be examined rather than the student learning. If, after identifying that a lesson has been implemented through quality curriculum and instruction, and 80% of students are not successful, reteaching or a different approach to teaching needs to be implemented. If a classroom behavior plan is in place and less than 80% of students are complying with the behavioral system, the system needs to be adjusted.

This also answers the age-old question about when it is time to move on with a new learning objective. If 80% of students have responded with success to the curriculum and instruction, it is time to move on in the instructional sequence. This does not mean a teacher should give up on the students who have not reached a level of success, but it does indicate the appropriate time to move forward with instruction. For instance, if students have received two weeks of quality instruction on addition of double-digit numbers and more than 80% of the class is now successful with the skill, it is time to move to the next skill. The ones who have not yet mastered the skill will continue to move on while receiving additional supports to accelerate their learning of double-digit addition.

This concept of 80% success is another way to gauge whether student needs are being met. If 80% are successful, then the system is working. If less than 80% are successful, the system is not working and needs to change.

RTI examines student performance, classroom conditions, instructional factors, and schoolwide structures.

One reason why RTI is so all-encompassing is that it addresses so many aspects of the educational system. It approaches student learning in and of itself as well as within the classroom environment. It also recognizes that the classroom environment is one part of a larger system of the whole school. RTI considers student learning as the product of the interaction between the learner and the curriculum as well as between the learner, the curriculum, and the instruction (see Figure 1.3).

Beyond this interaction, RTI acknowledges that the classroom is one element of the bigger system that comprises the school community. The classroom is influenced and impacted by the school as a whole, and these schoolwide influences affect not only the classroom, but the individual student as well (see Figure 1.4).

There are a few strong implications for the classroom teacher. The first is related to concepts of the whole-child approach. When considering a student's success or lack thereof, considerations extend beyond the responsibilities of the student to the teacher and the school. If students are exhibiting inappropriate behavior across a school, the schoolwide behavior system needs to be examined. The same holds true of a classroom. If most students in a classroom are struggling with learning a concept, rather than looking at each individual student as a separate entity, a look at the classroom instruction is needed.

The second implication embraces the concept that students' needs drive decision making. If a group of students is unsuccessful, the student

Figure 1.3   The Interactive Nature of Learning

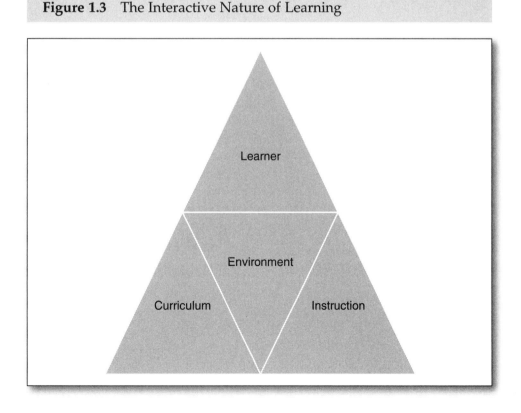

Figure 1.4   The Environment

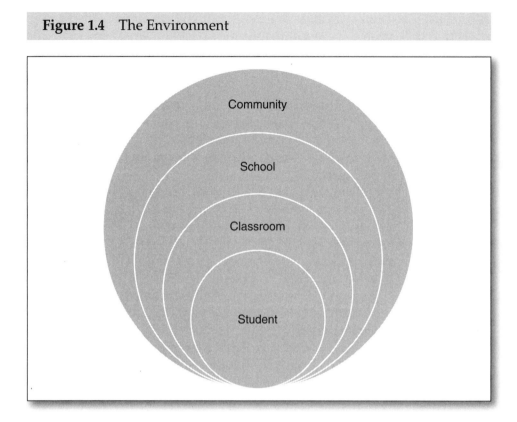

group must be examined in comparison to other student groups for the purpose of identifying student needs. They may be compared to other students within the same class, or the class as a whole may be compared with other classes. This comparison is done to target the variable that may be determining success or lack of success. RTI does not allow for a group of students to remain unsuccessful and become known as the "difficult class." RTI prompts the questions, "Why is a particular group of students unsuccessful while others are experiencing success?" and "What data help explain that occurrence?"

RTI expects that some students will need additional supports and services beyond the core curriculum and general behavioral expectations.

Not all students will be successful with the core instruction. Some will need additional supports and others additional challenges to show growth. While these statements seem obvious, RTI clearly communicates an expectation and acceptance of differences in students. Based on the 80% expectation of success, approximately 20% of students will need something in addition to the core curriculum and instruction. These students may need additional instruction, additional time for learning, or more intensity in the learning and instructional process. Behaviorally, these students may need a more tailored behavioral system in addition to the general classroom expectations and plan. For gifted students, there may be a need for additional enrichment or challenge. No matter what the need, RTI tells us that we cannot expect all students to always be successful with the core curriculum and instruction.

This principle extends the definition of quality instruction to include differentiated instruction as one component. It assures teachers that even with the best curriculum and highest-quality instruction in place, there will still be students who need more support in order to be successful. Simply stated, not all students will be successful all the time.

This is significant because the teacher no longer has to be all things to all students 100% of the time. This acknowledges the human factor and allows a teacher to be able to admit to not being able to reach an individual in a particular area without feeling like a failure. A standard has been set to recognize that there will be some students who will need more than the general education teacher, no matter how exemplary, is able to provide. This is a recognition of reality and not any failings on the part of the teacher.

A second strong factor is that the teacher must acknowledge when a practice is not working. If the pressure is taken off to expect 100% student success with instruction, then there is responsibility on the part of the teacher to acknowledge when instruction is not working. This requires data collection and communication. A teacher must be able to show what instruction was provided, how the typical students responded to that instruction, and then how a particular struggling student responded differently or not at all. The teacher is also responsible for communicating the needs of a student that go beyond what can be provided through the quality instruction at Tier 1. Once recognized, these needs cannot be pushed under the carpet; they need to be brought forward so that the additional supports and services can be put into place.

This principle also sets a standard for the teacher to recognize when there are large numbers of students who are unsuccessful, and it expects the teacher to respond to that information. If 60% of a group of students are unsuccessful with the instruction, RTI processes examine the instruction as opposed to the students. As professionals, teachers must be diligent in reflecting on practices using valid and reliable sources and methods to determine instructional effectiveness. Instructional strategies that may have once been effective may not work for a certain population. Again, this does not implicate the teacher as an unsuccessful educator but instead as a true professional. A doctor is not considered unsuccessful because he or she has a sick patient. The doctor is only considered deficient if he or she does not respond to the illness. The same is true with teachers. Students who fail to learn something do not reflect failure on the part of a teacher as long as the teacher is willing to treat and acknowledge the failure by attempting to correct it.

RTI provides a process for decision making based on clear data for every student.

At the heart of RTI is the practice of using data to make decisions. These decisions involve both instructional supports and behavioral supports, the amount of support to provide to a student, how intense the supports and services need to be, and what the supports and services themselves will look like. All of these decisions are based on data.

Data can be obtained in many forms: through observations as students work independently or in groups, through electronic response systems, and so on. Instructional strategies such as exit cards or a work sample also can provide the needed data. However, data can also be collected more formally. Standardized test results also provide data to help make decisions. Most helpful is the use of formative assessments that are done regularly. These assessments and the results from progress monitoring data together can best guide decision making.

The implications here are tied together. The first is that teachers need to examine data and become active collectors of data. The second is that, in many cases, teachers are already assessing students and possess a great deal of data needed as part of the instructional practice. Monitoring student progress is not a new concept. RTI tells us to continue this practice. While we may have used one source of data, or used the data for only one aspect of decision making, RTI requires data to be a central focus for all decisions.

RTI prescribes specific ways to look at student data when using these data for decision making. One way RTI encourages examining data is by reflecting on trends as a whole. These may be trends of a district, a school, a grade level, a classroom, a group of students, or an individual. Looking at trends enables needs to become more apparent, and connections that may not have been seen before are made. Trend examination also allows educators to discuss rates of learning and levels of mastery. This becomes pivotal when addressing the needs of a struggling learner as well as predicting future performance. RTI also encourages examining data in relation to clearly stated expectations. By establishing a level of expectation, an aim line provides a reference point for any data set. Finally, RTI directs educators to examine data in relation to other learners, not just on standardized testing but on a more frequent basis. Data reflecting the level of understanding in response to instruction can be compared from one student who has received the instruction to another student who has received the same instruction.

By using data for comparisons and trend analysis, the teacher's emphasis on data in the classroom shifts from simply a student's level of mastery on a particular concept to the classroom itself, the environment, the curriculum and instruction, as well as the learners. Instead of only comparing a student's performance to a benchmark, student performance is compared through several lenses for a better indicator of both performance and progress. Data examined in this way open the door to additional probing in order to establish needs. For instance, if a whole group of students in a particular class are struggling in a certain aspect, the data suggest that the curriculum or instruction is in need of change, rather than the students. On the other hand, if a student shows performance well below his or her peers and has received the same instruction as peers, data suggest looking more deeply at that individual student's need. Data examined by looking at trends can also suggest when environmental factors may be coming into play. For instance, data may show that large numbers of students perform poorly on Fridays in comparison to other days. Rather than looking at isolated scores or data from a particular student, RTI prompts a further and broader examination of data. Besides the details, a big picture can be painted through the use of data.

RTI requires continuous progress monitoring and formative assessments to drive instruction.

When determining the degree of success a student is experiencing, RTI strongly emphasizes the need to go beyond gut instincts and instinctive decision making. Throughout history, educators have not always been accurate in identifying certain student qualities and yet have used these gut instincts to make instructional decisions and even initiate processes to label students based on intuition. RTI requires instructional and educational decisions to be based on data. For the past 20 years, progress monitoring and data collection efforts have been recognized as effective practice (NASDSE, 2006).

In RTI, decision making is done constantly through a model of clear steps that include identifying a problem, creating a hypothesis about why the problem exists, implementing an intervention, and then monitoring the effects of that intervention. This monitoring is done through the use of data and becomes a key component. If something is not working, it does not continue unnoticed and unaddressed.

At all tiers, data from assessment provide the stage for understanding student needs and responding to those needs. Screening assessment data provide a big picture and are used to get an idea of how a student or group of students is doing overall in comparison to others or a norm. It is a snapshot and acts as a thermometer to potentially provide a quick measure of levels of success and need (Brown-Chidsey, Bronaugh, & McGraw, 2009). These screening assessments may be formal or informal in nature and are often summative assessments, indicating what the student has already learned or can do. Diagnostic data provide more specific information and are used to pinpoint targeted areas of strength or need. These assessments also take on a variety of formats and are administered to gain more specific insight. Diagnostics require cause-effect thinking about both teacher and student performance. "If a student does X, I will respond with this" or "If I use this for an instructional method, the student will do X" (Gregory & Kuzmich, 2004). Certainly, this is at the heart of the meaning of the term *response* in RTI.

One hallmark of RTI is the practice of systematic progress monitoring. This too requires the same cause-effect thinking as does diagnostic assessment. Progress monitoring is the careful and consistent collection of data for the purpose of identifying trends, patterns, and rates of learning. There are several reasons to use progress monitoring. One important reason is that the data will reflect the effectiveness of instruction and indicate whether strategies are working (National Center on Response to Intervention, n.d.-a). Another reason to use continual progress monitoring is so that parents and students can see progress. Students who are aware of their progress are more likely to work harder in order to make gains toward goals (Safer & Fleischman, 2005). A final reason is that progress monitoring is done frequently so that changes to instruction are implemented in more effective, efficient ways. Progress monitoring leads to more timely responsiveness to instruction. Progress monitoring is also tied to formative assessment: the collection of data for the purpose of instructional decision making. It is intended to *form* instruction and not just *inform*. Together, progress monitoring and formative assessment provide the information and guide the decision-making processes of instruction.

RTI requires the continuous collection of data in order to determine student progress. Data are collected for students as individuals, for a classroom as a whole, and even for an entire grade level. Data are used to identify trends and patterns in student performance. Beyond the need for continuous progress monitoring, RTI demands that instructional decisions be based on student performance data rather than instinct-based, one-time assessments or assumptions about a student or group of students. Data from progress monitoring and formative assessments drive decision-making practices.

RTI responds to learner needs when they are recognized, and intervention comes without labels.

RTI emphasizes early intervention. Rather than waiting for a student to fail and then waiting while procedures qualify a student for services, RTI promotes early action. Providing rigorous interventions at a young age before the student has fallen too far behind can turn the process around and allow the student to become proficient. Without early interventions, a small gap at a young age grows over time and becomes a significant barrier to success in later grades.

However, early intervention does not just mean providing interventions to students at a young age. It also means that interventions occur immediately when a need is recognized and not only after testing processes and labels are assigned. RTI emphasizes the urgency to provide supports and services to any student who needs them when the need arises rather than only when a student "qualifies" for additional services. In the past, we provided additional supports and services after a student was referred and identified as qualifying for special education services. For instance, students who had a severe discrepancy between achievement and intellectual ability were provided with supports and services through the special education process and were assured these services through an IEP. Students who had a significantly low IQ score or significant behavior or emotional disabilities also were provided supports and services through special education. Students who did not fall into a category designated as an area of special education were left to chance in hopes that a teacher would recognize needs and meet those needs within the daily instruction. The RTI model ensures that all students receive supports and services if it is clear that there is a need. A student does not have to wait for the often lengthy process of referral for evaluations, followed by evaluations and a possible label in the special education system, before receiving the help needed. RTI moves us from a "wait to fail" model to a responsive and proactive model. Now, IDEIA allows an approach to identification that can be made by looking at whether a child responds to research-based interventions as expected by defensible research. This requires the teacher to be constantly monitoring and assessing students in order to determine these needs.

This is one of the most significant changes in educational practices from the past. Instead of a model in which the goal was to give a struggling student a label, now the goal is to get the struggling learner the needed services and supports. Instead of asking, "What is wrong with this student?" the question becomes "What can we do to support the student's performance and help promote success?" Time and efforts are directed toward what we can do to help rather than what we can find wrong. Although individualized testing may still be done within RTI, the purpose of the testing becomes one of gaining more information about the student's thinking processes rather than qualifying for a service. This takes priority over efforts to qualify the student to receive a label and then, in turn, receive supports and services.

Another strong implication for the teacher is that RTI requires collaboration and joint effort for achieving success. All students are everyone's responsibility. It is expected that general education teachers, special education teachers, and teachers from multiple content areas will work together to meet the needs of each student. Collaboration becomes a requirement. While collaboration does present challenges, such as finding time, there are great advantages to professionals coming together to bring in an array of expertise (Murawski, 2005). Teachers have exhausting demands placed on them in terms of curriculum and instruction. They have been expected to be both content area experts in multiple fields as well as experts in instructional strategies and practices. RTI demands differentiated instruction by them and collaboration with other professionals in order to meet student needs.

RTI strives to go beyond students making some gains to students making accelerated gains at a rate that will allow them to not fall further behind.

Over the past decade or more, the educational system has focused on measuring student achievement in terms of growth as compared from one year to the next. If a student reflected on assessments that he or she was making gains, there was no more that needed to be done. RTI, along with other accountability initiatives, changes that. Now student growth is viewed in terms of the amount of growth over a period of time. The pace at which a student is making gains has become as important as whether he or she is making gains. When a student struggles and falls further behind, it is even more essential to collect data in order to monitor the learning rate. The further behind a student is, the faster the student needs to learn in order to catch up. This is done by supplementing the core instruction with additional supports and services rather than supplanting the core instruction. In that supplemental support, the goal is not just to maintain the current rate at which the student is learning but to actually accelerate the learning for the student to catch up to peers.

In the past, remediation services functioned to replace the core instruction in many cases. A student received different instruction than his or her peers. This often increased gaps in the student's achievement levels as compared to his or her peers. Even if learning reflected progress, it was often at the same rate as peers in general education classes, and therefore the gap was maintained. Progress was monitored and success was defined as a student showing gains in performance.

RTI redefines success as student performance that reflects accelerated gains, at a pace more rapid than peers, for the purpose of shrinking the gap between the struggling student's performance and that of peers. This acceleration is the purpose for the increased intensity and implementation of supports and services. The underlying principle is that a student will be able to achieve more if strategic, systematic, research-based supports and services are in place and matched to the learner. For instance, if a particular student is struggling with learning sight words and peers are learning at a rate of four new words per week, in order to catch up the struggling student needs to learn the four that the peers are learning as well as additional words from past weeks. Based on the rates of learning and how far behind the student is in relation to peers, the number of additional words per week can be determined. The expectation is that with additional supports, the student can learn more or at an accelerated rate than his or her peers in order to be back on the same level with the peers.

This concept raises great levels of discussion around the expectations of students and learning. For those teachers who say that it is unrealistic to expect a struggling learner to learn at a rate faster than peers who are not struggling, there is one question to be asked: Can the student ever have a chance to catch up to peers and close the gap any other way? In the past, we maintained the struggling student's position in relation to peers by supplanting instruction. For instance, the student may have learned four different words than the peers. Even at the rate of four words per week, if there has been a gap, a gap will remain. If, however, the student learned the four words per week that the peers were learning and was supported with learning those four with additional supports to learn two more words per week through the more intensive services received, it is possible for the gap to close. Without this approach, it is not possible to close the gap. We must give every student the chance to be successful. There has been talk in education for a long time about closing the achievement gap, and now here is where the rubber meets the road. RTI makes the change needed for the gap to ever have a possibility of being closed.

This principle also puts a heavy weight on teachers in the younger grades. It requires teachers to use data to quickly identify any area in which a student is falling behind peers. The sooner the gap is recognized and addressed, the smaller the gap is. Gone unnoticed, a student who continues to fall behind can quickly become a full year of achievement behind peers. Research tells us that performance at early elementary levels has a direct correlation to high school performance. Like a water leak in a concrete wall, a small drip that is noticed and addressed has a much more desirable outcome than a pinhole ignored until the drip becomes a gushing hole. In blunt terms, the sooner needs are recognized and addressed, the less damage is done.

RTI includes aspects beyond the instructional time and considers the student as a whole child.

This principle reflects the changing times in our educational system. It breaks down the barriers of a learning environment as being contained within four walls. It recognizes that learning happens in all settings and in all parts of a student's life. This principle also reflects the relationship of schools with community and resources beyond the school building. It acknowledges that parents have a role to play in students' education, both as collaborative partners and as contributing factors toward success. It stems from the outreach that now exists between homes, schools, and community organizations and businesses. RTI addresses the whole child and, in doing so, opens the door for a bigger picture of the student.

In the past, educators were cautious in blending the services provided within the school and those funded through outside sources. In meetings in the past, little consideration was given for any additional supports or services that a student was receiving outside of the public educational system. This was, in large part, due to funding issues. A public school could only address areas in which the public school received funding. Afterschool programs or private tutoring were often completely separate and not even considered in discussions.

Now, when considering the supports and services of a student, educators can look beyond what is happening in the classroom. Before- and afterschool programs, tutoring programs, and other supports can be discussed and considered as avenues to help support student success. The perspective has shifted from an 8:30–3:30 lens to a 24/7 one. RTI encourages parents to get involved and allows them to take some ownership in supporting student needs. Educators look at the whole child rather than just what occurs within the school day.

RTI requires collaboration not only with educational professionals but also with a variety of other people as well. If supports from the outside are going to be most beneficial to a student, they need to be streamlined and seamless. All stakeholders should have common goals and be moving in the same direction. Teachers will need to communicate and collaborate with outside tutors, afterschool programs, and even private tutoring businesses. Teachers may teach parents how to provide additional supports for the student. Together, information and data are to be shared. Progress can be tracked in order to identify both growth and effectiveness of all the supports and services. RTI creates a demand for collaboration not just within the educational system and school building but with the outside community as well. Problem solving also becomes a shared responsibility and not one solely placed on the teacher. A teacher is no longer isolated in having responsibility for a student's education. RTI acknowledges and honors the old saying that it takes a village to raise a child. Indeed, it supports and reinforces that idea.

SUMMARY

RTI is a systematic framework designed to provide students with the supports and services needed in order to be successful in the classroom. While there still remain some inconsistencies within RTI, there are also some guiding principles in common to all RTI practices. Each of these principles has direct application for and impact on the classroom teacher. Central to the framework is a classroom that provides consistent, research-based, high-quality instruction. From here, all decisions regarding supports and services evolve from the responsiveness of the student to the curriculum and instruction. These decisions are systematic and driven by data and evidence. Early responses to student needs are critical in order to implement remediation before the gap becomes a chasm. Services are provided when needed as opposed to when directed by a label or law. RTI touches on almost all other educational initiatives and supports the central premise that the students themselves are at the heart of education.

QUESTIONS TO CONSIDER

- How is the process of RTI similar to what was done in the past to support student needs? How is this process new and different in its approach?
- When considering the framework of RTI, about which aspects can you say, "I already do that"? What evidence do you have that reflects this?
- How do you see the framework being different for behavior than for academics?
- How do you see students identified as gifted fitting into this framework?
- Where do you see overlap between behavior and academics?
- What assessments are being implemented to identify student needs earlier on?
- What systems are in place to support the needed time and forum for collaboration with other professionals?
- What strengths do you see in using the RTI framework within the educational system?
- What challenges do you see presented by this framework?
- Which principles of RTI do you feel most strongly about?

2

Principles of DI and Implications in the Classroom

We must no longer simply acknowledge differences in the classroom. We must respond to those differences. As Sidney Jourard said, "there is no biological, geographical, social, economic, or psychological determiner in man's condition that he cannot transcend if he is suitably invited or challenged to do so."

WHAT IS DIFFERENTIATED INSTRUCTION?

Differentiated instruction (DI) is the systematic planning and implementation process for creating educational experiences tailored to meet the needs of each individual, honoring and celebrating differences by capitalizing on strengths and supporting needs. It is student centered, with learning opportunities intentionally designed to foster the highest achievement for each student (O'Meara, 2010). DI is not a singular linear process but is instead a multidirectional process with critical junctures and decisions. It is a process used in planning as well as in teaching.

Why is differentiating instruction so critical? Each day it becomes more apparent that the classroom is changing to include greater spectrums of diversity. We see great diversity in appearances, values, cultures, learning habits, supports from family and community, academic abilities, and experiences, to name just a few. It is also more and more apparent these days that teachers are responsible for honoring the integrity of the curriculum and its standards while striving to guide each child to meet his or her highest potential as a learner. Therefore, educators must focus efforts on both best teaching practices in curriculum and instruction as well as meeting the diverse needs of learners in their classrooms (Gregory & Kuzmich, 2004).

In this age of accountability, administrators often ask, "What does differentiation look like in the classroom? How do I know if I am seeing it?" Unfortunately, there is no checklist that can be provided to say, "If you see _____, you are seeing differentiated instruction." One of the main reasons for this is because DI is entirely dependent upon the planning and preparation of the instruction. The delivery that is observed is the result of that work. DI is about systematically planning instruction based on established standards combined with what is known about the students and their relationship to those standards. It also involves the planning that is done in order to be prepared for the varied responses of students to the content during the learning process (see Figure 2.1).

Figure 2.1   The "Behind the Scenes" Look of Differentiated Instruction

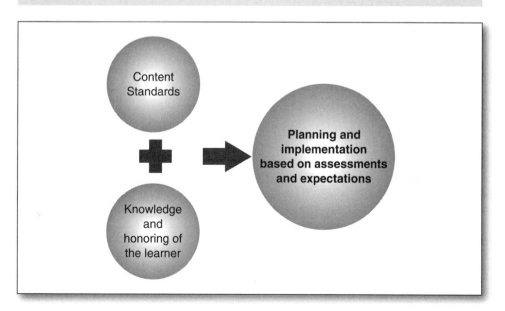

DI IN ACTION

Ms. Beal was implementing a lesson with her third-grade students focused on the relationship between multiplication and area as part of an introduction to what multiplication is. She knew her students well, having examined results of universal screenings. She had also been teaching them for the past three months. She thought about her students as individuals and as a whole group when she planned her instructional approach. Ms. Beal's desired learning outcome was for all students to understand the concept of multiplication as repeated sets of the same quantity uniting to form an area made up of the initial quantity by the number of repeated sets. To introduce this lesson, she had students create repeated sets of numbers using cubes. Each student created four sets of three cubes. They counted by 3s using the cubes to get to 12, with Ms. Beal modeling using her document camera. She then had them create an area using the 12 cubes and asked them to discuss with a partner ways to describe their shape in number forms. Besides saying 12 cubes, some students were able to determine that the area was also four sets of three or sets of three, four times. Ms. Beal wrote the algorithm for the students as $3 \times 4 = 12$. She then used a scaffolded approach to repeat the process with four sets of five cubes. She provided verbal and visual guidance for some students while allowing others to work ahead of her pace. Ms. Beal knew some students would be very challenged by this lesson. For those students, she had prepared mats with the outlines of both the sets of cubes and the areas on graph paper. She provided a counting line to assist these students with skip counting. For one student with fine motor control difficulties, Ms. Beal had the cubes already formed into groups of three.

Ms. Beal also knew that some students knew their multiplication facts already, but she was unsure if they understood the concept. While continuing with her main lesson, she challenged these five students to use the cubes and show her what 4×6 looked like and determine how that was the same as or different than 6×4. Two students were highly advanced in math. Ms. Beal paired them together and at the beginning of the lesson challenged them to create their models as cubes rather than as area. Their cubes were areas of four by four stacked four high. She allowed them to explore different numbers to determine any patterns they could. When this group time was complete, Ms. Beal brought the class back together to reflect on their learning. Some students shared that repeated sets of numbers were the same as multiplication. Others shared that these sets put together always create rectangles. The two students working on three-dimensional cubes reported that the patterns continued upward as well through repeated addition and modeled $3 \times 4 = 12$ and layering resulted in 24, 36, and so on.

In planning, Ms. Beal predicted students' response and the levels of supports they would need to be successful. When she delivered her lesson, she provided those supports. Her teaching was like the conducting of an orchestra. She was able to teach to the whole class while addressing individual needs. Through careful planning, she was prepared to meet the students where they were in relation to the expectation. Her delivery of instruction reflected careful planning, and as a result, Ms. Beal was able to meet students with a variety of needs, all working toward established desired learning outcomes.

The term *differentiated instruction* has been around since the 1950s and '60s, although the interpretations and definitions have evolved through the years. Currently, it is commonly understood through definitions that reflect principles related to the process of adapting learning experiences to meet the needs of different learners. All definitions agree that differentiation is not just a philosophy but also a practice of meeting students' needs. This practice is seen in adjustments made within three broad aspects: content, process, and product (Tomlinson, 2003). Alterations to instruction are designed to support and challenge all learners. Decision making is done through consistent assessment before, during, and in response to the learning process. The assessment and instruction are seamless.

Within these three areas of instruction, several aspects can be considered when differentiating instruction. Any one of those aspects may be adjusted to take into account the learner's ability, background knowledge, interests, motivators, learning habits, pace of work, preferred learning environment, or other factors that impact student learning. These may be considered and assessed in isolation, or multiple aspects may be considered at any one time. Differentiation requires an assessment of any number of aspects to determine who the learner is in relation to what is being learned.

PRINCIPLES OF DIFFERENTIATION

DI is responsive.

A teacher who is differentiating instruction is responsive to students and their needs as well as the context within which the students are learning. The best lesson in the world with high-level thinking required of the students is still not the best lesson if it occurs the period before a pep rally. The best lesson is one that takes into account the students, the learning objectives, and the environment.

DI is centered on students and their relationship to the learning.

DI does not start and end with the textbook or the content. It considers the desired learning outcome and the learners who will be interacting with this content. Together, the decisions and process itself become the dance of these two elements. Both have an equal part in taking the lead and following throughout the dance. The interactions are dynamic and direct the movement.

DI is based on assessment.

DI requires knowledge of and response to the student in relation to the material being learned. Adjustments to instruction are made based on the way students interact with the material. Student assessment in any number of aspects related to learning is critical.

Differentiation requires a focus on the big picture as opposed to isolated skills.

DI is more than providing accommodations, scaffolding, or pacing. It is the work that goes into the pre-lesson preparation as well as the ongoing and continuous response to each student's learning process. It goes beyond an acceptance of differences to an expectation of differences. It prepares to honor those differences through learning interactions.

Differentiation includes all those principles stated along with a systematic and intentional process designed to meet the needs of each learner. In order to accomplish that end, multiple considerations and practices must be implemented. Differentiation is much more than a collection of teaching strategies, materials, or mandates. It is a process that involves the curriculum, the instruction, the instructor, the learner, and the relationship of those elements as evidenced through assessment. Figure 2.2 provides an outline of the steps in the DI process.

Steps 1 and 2: Identify the standards and their relationship to each other.

The first step of DI is to determine the content to be learned as defined by the standards and objectives. The standard or objective should be clearly defined in such a way that there is a complete understanding of the expectation for what a student should know or be able to do. For over two decades, this idea of beginning with the end in mind has been a best practice for all elements in life involving goal setting (Covey, 1990). Without clarity of the desired learning outcome, it is not possible to systematically adapt learning experiences and instruction, and any attempts at differentiating become random attempts to provide variety.

For example, if students are given the task of writing a five-paragraph essay and the objectives are not clear, adaptations made for a student could compromise his or her learning. If the objective is for the student to indicate an understanding of cell reproduction through the essay, then providing an option to create a graphic representation would not compromise the learning. However, if the objective is related to the writing

Figure 2.2   The Process of Differentiated Instruction

Step 1: Examine the standards and objectives to be taught. Determine the type of knowledge demanded of each standard and/or objective.

Step 2: Establish the conceptual understanding related to the facts and skills required.

Step 3: For any fact or skill, determine the level of fluency needed for mastery.

Step 4: Design independent student activities that address the facts and skills to be addressed along with accommodations for students who need support in achieving mastery of the facts and skills.

Step 5: Reflect on personal knowledge and attitudes related to resources, the content, and the students.

Step 6: Pre-assess students in the areas of knowledge of facts, skills, conceptual understandings, experiences, attitudes, motivations, and ideas.

Step 7: Determine strategies for instruction at different levels of cognitive processing to include concrete, representational, and abstract processes.

Step 8: Determine the flow of classroom activities to include individual, small-group, and whole-group instruction.

Step 9: Determine benchmarks of student performance, and develop tools for ongoing measurement of progress.

Step 10: Develop selections and criteria for the summative product or performance that accurately reflects the intended outcomes of the unit.

Source: O'Meara, 2010.

process itself, allowing the student to create a graphic would compromise the learning. If the objective is not clear, the entire purpose of the activity may be defeated.

In addition to having a clear objective, it is also important to consider the depth of thinking required for the objective. As early as the 1950s, Ralph Tyler established the notion that different types of learning require different types of teaching (Madaus & Stufflebeam, 1989). Later, Hilda Taba made that concept more clear and applicable when she provided names for categories of knowledge or types of learning. Following are Taba's types of knowledge:

- Facts: Something that can be known as true or false
- Skills: The application of facts
- Concepts: The product resulting from related facts and skills
- Principles: Concepts merged with other concepts into broader understandings
- Generalizations: Principles merged together into big ideas (Tomlinson et al., 2002, p. 92)

Many times the standards are written with the prefix "The student will know" or "The student will do." These indicate standards centered on facts and skills. In many cases, standards also consider conceptual understandings. It is rare that standards are elevated to the height of principles or generalizations. When examining the standards to be addressed, it is important to recognize the level of knowledge involved. The ones written as facts and skills allow for fewer opportunities to differentiate. Facts and skills lend themselves to the practice of scaffolding with the use of accommodations to provide different levels of support and challenge. Scaffolding is the practice of providing the necessary supports for a student to experience success in a challenging situation (Tomlinson, 2003). However, facts and skills cannot be differentiated to the same degree as conceptual understandings and higher levels of knowledge. For instance, there are a limited number of ways that one can provide instruction on a skill such as hammering a nail; however, there are many more ways to provide instruction on joining two pieces of wood. Therefore, as Ralph Tyler established long ago, conceptual standards must be treated differently than those at the level of facts and skills. This distinction between the facts and skills and conceptual understandings is of critical importance not only in DI but also within the Response to Intervention framework.

A final consideration regarding the examination of the standards involves the relationship of the standards to each other. Appropriate instructional design often includes multiple standards addressed in conjunction with each other. For instance, a standard determining that students use context cues to identify the meaning of unknown words may be embedded within lessons that contain other standards as well. Within each content area, there are many standards that serve as a foundation for other standards. Therefore, when planning instruction, there is most often a need to combine more than one standard to form a relationship between the learning objectives.

The consideration of the relationship between standards and bringing them together under a theme or big idea has many advantages. The most important advantage is that it assists learners in making connections and developing schema. This allows learners to transfer and apply their new understandings rather than simply retain the information in isolation. There is increased understanding and more potential for application in real-world experiences (Wiggins & McTighe, 2005).

Many learners struggle to make sense of new learning or connect it to what is already known. Learning becomes memorization of random facts and ideas. With the practice of establishing a relationship of the standards to each other, students are provided with an organizational structure to make sense of their learning. For example, if a science teacher is speaking about chlorophyll, when we hear that term our brains may bring up an image of a leaf and the sun. This image helps us connect chlorophyll to plants in general and systems of energy. These thoughts that we generate from hearing the term *chlorophyll* can only happen if the information we possess about chlorophyll has been stored properly in our brains. We are able to reflect on what we know and make connections in order to make sense of what the science teacher is saying. However, if that term has been stored randomly, we may not be able to access that information from our stored ideas and will be lost in anything being said about chlorophyll. Instead, we may be thinking the teacher is talking about two people, Chlor and Phil, and generate very different and unrelated thoughts.

Therefore, by providing a framework for the organization of thought, a student is able to assimilate new learning with what is already known. This will assist not only with recall but also with the ability to make other connections. This practice of explicitly making these connections has become more evident even in the way standards are written. Many are organized around a big idea that will assist with the connection to other content areas as well. For instance, a mathematics standard from the past expressed a learning objective involving converting decimals into fractions. This is simply a skill. However, the new Focal Points from the National Council for Teachers of Mathematics (2006) standard now reads that, in addition to a general understanding of decimals, students should develop an understanding of the connections between fractions and decimals. This understanding of the relationship rather than simply the calculation is much more conceptually based than the past skill-based standard.

Steps 3 and 4: Define the level of mastery to be achieved, and develop practice opportunities with related accommodations to support or challenge learners.

It is important to determine what mastery looks like at the onset of instructional planning. This is necessary so that there is a clear target and so that indicators can be developed to know when that target has been reached. It also provides a vehicle for a coordinated effort focused on increased achievement (Tucker & Codding, 1998). This identification and clarity of mastery is also important in the process when accommodations are considered. Without clear knowledge of the end goal, instruction can easily become aimless and random. By explicitly defining the desired learning outcome and the criteria, the DI process remains systematic and effective. It also emphasizes teaching to established standards rather than randomly providing opportunities and activities for learning to possibly occur.

For example, a teacher has assigned students to create a relief map of the world using materials to reflect elevation. She has required them to label the continents and main bodies of water. She has also required that students include a compass to show direction. When asked why she is doing this activity, the teacher replies that it is a fun way to learn geography. She mentions students being able to identify the continents and directions on a compass but says nothing about elevation concepts. Although the project may be enjoyable and students may learn the names of the continents, the teacher has a lack of clarity as to what learning objectives she wants to address through the activity. With this activity-based approach, learning is hit or miss. Additionally, supports are difficult to design or determine as appropriate. When asked if a student would be allowed to create the map using animation software on the computer, the teacher is not sure if that would be appropriate or fair. When asked if the map could be provided and students could just add the labels, again she is not sure. Without clear expectations of the learning outcome, appropriate supports cannot be implemented to address different learners' needs.

Accommodations provided for the learning of facts and skills are different than those for conceptual development. Accommodations for these types of learning are designed for struggling learners but not provided to challenge above-level learners. If mastery is reached and more challenge is needed, rather than providing accommodations to increase the challenge, accelerated learning should be implemented so that the learner is introduced to new challenges. For the struggling learner, accommodations can be provided in multiple areas. Materials such as manipulatives, software, rulers, highlighters, and self-correcting products may be provided to assist a struggling learner in practice. The process of the learning of facts and skills may be adjusted through the use of such things as mnemonic devices, visuals and pictures, graphic organizers, and short cuts (O'Meara, 2010).

Finally, it is important to clearly define mastery in order to establish benchmarks or measures of progress toward the goal. Without knowing where one is going, it is impossible to know how much further there is to travel. A teacher who wants students to name and label the continents on a map can identify how close or far a student is from mastery based on the performance while learning. A teacher who wants students to learn about maps and continents cannot tell how close or far any student is from mastering maps and continents.

Once mastery of the facts and skills is defined, the next aspect of this step is to develop opportunities for information to be practiced and reinforced. Facts and skills must be practiced and reinforced for them to become fluent and applicable. Practice opportunities should remain largely independent for learners, with teacher monitoring being more prevalent than instructing. Homework and the use of technology provide avenues for independent practice to occur.

Step 5: Assess self.

The next step of DI is to formally or informally complete a self-assessment related to the content and the learners. The following are some questions to ask before continuing with the DI process:

Are the student expectations in relation to the standard challenging and yet not overly frustrating?

Do I thoroughly understand the content? Can I explain the content in more than one way?

Are there connections that can be made with other content or standards that the students have mastered?

Are there connections to real-world experiences?

Do I have the necessary resources to meet a variety of learning styles and levels of ability?

It is as important for the teacher to pre-assess his or her own personal beliefs as it is to assess student beliefs. The assessment is not intended to be judgmental but instead to inventory factors that will affect the delivery of instruction. By completing a self-assessment related to the content and the learners, a teacher can avoid common pitfalls and become more motivating as an instructor (Shalaway, 2005).

Step 6: Assess students.

The next step is to gather information about the learners in relation to the outcome that has been established. This is the pre-assessment. There are countless ways to pre-assess students in any number of domains. These domains include their current levels of knowledge, related ideas, background, interest, or work habits and preferences. The specific role of the pre-assessment is to identify the starting point for instruction and build from that point. The pre-assessment drives the initial instruction. It is the first critical point at which the teacher is responsive to the students' information. A pre-assessment can illuminate personal beliefs, misconceptions, and deficits as well as areas in which students may already exceed the objective. A well-designed pre-assessment offers opportunities to individually share facts, skills, and concepts related to the topic or learning objective. The pre-assessment should be open-ended to provide as much opportunity as possible for students to communicate their related thoughts. Figure 2.3 lists some pre-assessment tools.

Pre-Assessments for Study and Work Habits

There are several surveys that ask students to complete phrases to indicate preferred learning styles. These are often used to target students' indicated preferences of learning through visual, auditory, or kinesthetic modalities. There are also surveys that target specific areas of preference

Figure 2.3   Pre-Assessment Tools

Word sort or word shuffles	Students are provided with terms that they know and that are related to the topic to be studied. They arrange the words into categories as they see appropriate.
Prediction activities	Students are given a situation and asked to make a prediction and justify the prediction.
Quadrant charts to indicate multiple aspects of a topic	Students are given four quadrants and attributes to write in each quadrant. The attributes can be any related features. They may include similarities in one box, differences in another, definitions in a third. and details in the fourth.
Brainstormed lists	Students brainstorm everything they know or believe about a topic in a list format.

within the construct of multiple intelligences (Gardner, 1993). It is also not uncommon at the beginning of a school year or semester for students to be asked to complete surveys indicating personal work habits such as how and when they study, if they like noise or quiet when studying, and study skills. It is much less important which tool is used and more important that the information gained from the tool is actually used for planning instruction. Too often, these surveys are completed, discussed with students, and filed away for the semester. The information provided by students on these surveys should be used to guide the development of learning activities (Dawkins, 2010).

SCENARIO

Ms. Bell provided a survey to her class that was geared toward multiple intelligences. She discovered that several boys in her class preferred visual-spatial activities rather than linguistic ones. She also discovered that she had several students who indicated preference toward kinesthetic learning activities. As Ms. Bell created her geography lessons, she kept this valuable information in mind. In the past, she had taught vocabulary related to geographic terms by providing the terms and discussing each definition as the students wrote or drew definitions of their own. With the information she had about her current students' learning preferences, Ms. Bell tailored her approach. Some students explored a set of pictures and video clips showing each term. Others used software to show where on the globe the particular feature was found. A third group of students created a hand or arm movement to represent the terms. Each group shared their learning with each other, and only afterward were students asked to write notes about the meaning of each term.

Pre-Assessments for Related Ideas and Background

Pre-assessment surveys of background knowledge target students' conceptual understandings of a content area gained through experiences the students have had. Again, after gaining this insight, the information must be used to develop the instruction. It would be a shame if Ms. Bell was teaching about the Smoky Mountains and had a student who had lived in these mountains for several years but never deviated from the instruction to acknowledge this. She might ask that student to share with the class. Ms. Bell could also adjust her instruction to continue to challenge students who may already know about the Smoky Mountains with an extension activity while providing others with more support in their learning.

To meet the needs of the student who has already exceeded the learning objectives related to the Smoky Mountains, Ms. Bell could design an enrichment activity. While other students are identifying characteristics unique to this mountain range, Ms. Bell would ask this student to select a different mountain range and compare it to the Smoky Mountain range. It is the practice of using the information about students that creates the purpose and value of the pre-assessment.

Pre-Assessments for Interest and Motivation

This is typically the least common aspect given attention on a pre-assessment, yet student motivation can determine the success or failure of a learning experience. A student who is motivated or empowered is likely to learn more than one who is unmotivated (Miller & Desberg, 2009). Motivation-based pre-assessments are designed to identify particular aspects of a content area that spark interest with a student. Again, these tend to be completed at the beginning of a year or semester as a "getting to know you" activity but often are filed away and not used in instructional decision making. Yet the knowledge about students' interests can assist in creating meaningful learning experiences in the classroom.

SCENARIO

At the start of the year, Mrs. Levere asked students to complete a survey about their preferences, hobbies, and interests. She found that a large number of students enjoyed skateboarding and nature. Mrs. Levere, who teaches science, uses this information as often as possible. She has redesigned her lessons around students' interests. In the physics unit, instead of creating an invention using properties of physics, the students are creating a skate park with an obstacle course. When teaching classification and systems, Mrs. Levere based the unit not on the traditional scientific systems, but on the design and organization

(Continued)

(Continued)

of a mall and its different types of stores to parallel the scientific classification system. She also gives students the option of creating a classification system for cars rather than mall stores. Mrs. Levere used students' areas of interest to help make their learning experiences more meaningful and applicable.

Pre-Assessment of Current Knowledge Levels

This is the most commonly assessed aspect of pre-assessment. Students complete a pretest on the actual content that they will be learning as well as possibly some prerequisite skills or facts needed. This type of pre-assessment provides insight into a starting point for the instruction. The information often reveals what gaps or foundational skills are lacking as well as misinformation that students may have. It also provides a vehicle to identify any students who have already mastered what is going to be taught. Pre-assessing current knowledge levels focuses on the content and curriculum. This type of assessment may be used in conjunction with another assessment that focuses more on providing instructional insight.

SCENARIO

Mr. Weiss teaches math and administered a pre-assessment on fractions prior to teaching objectives that include adding and subtracting mixed numbers. He asked students to name fractions from pictorial representations, add and subtract simple fractions with like denominators, add and subtract fractions with unlike denominators, and add and subtract mixed numbers. There were 10 items in all. What Mr. Weiss discovered was that while all students could add and subtract fractions with like denominators, there were a few students who could not correctly name fractional parts from a picture and a few who could not add and subtract fractions with unlike denominators. He also discovered that three students could already meet his learning objective of adding and subtracting mixed numbers. With this information, Mr. Weiss created small groups and provided remediation to students at their level of need. He also grouped the three students who showed mastery of the objective and provided enrichment and additional challenges for them.

Step 7: Develop strategies for instruction at different levels or different perspectives of the content matched to the learner.

We have seen in the scenarios how, after identifying students' strengths and areas of needed support, the teacher then reacts to that information by providing instruction and supports to learners that match the instructional content and process to their learning needs. While Step 6 focuses on the learner needs, this step focuses on the differentiation of content and the learning process. Learning activities can be adjusted within any one of those areas. These decisions are, of course, based on information about the students gained through both formal and informal assessments.

Content

When one refers to the differentiation of content, in many cases the differentiation actually refers to either the materials or a particular perspective of the content. It does not generally refer to the student expectations or learning outcomes. The standard sets the expectations, and the standard remains intact. This is a critical distinction. The standard itself does not change with the process of DI. The standard remains the same, although the approaches to the standard may be different and adjusted for different learners. Standards exist in order to establish a common understanding of the expectations of students in terms of academic success. The standards determine what to teach, but not how to teach (Fisher & Frey, 2001).

For instance, when Mrs. Levere was teaching her physics unit, she adjusted the content for different students by addressing their interests. This was done to help motivate students and enable them to make connections to their lives. Some of the students in her class were designing a skate park, while others were designing humane animal traps for rescue. All learning was directed toward specific principles of physics as determined by the standards. However, Mrs. Levere adjusted the content or representative topics that included the standards to better meet the needs of her students by providing varied approaches.

Process

The learning process can also be differentiated through different approaches to the objectives. This is the result of careful planning. The differentiation of the learning process allows for students to process material though different venues that best meet their strengths and needs. For some learners, this may be by looking at pictures to process the information. Other students may need to read about the content to make sense of it. Still others may need to hear it and then talk about it with another learner to gain understanding. Watching video clips, using manipulatives, drawing, designing, hearing, and touching are all different ways in which students may process knowledge. The decision about what learning processes to provide is based on the student's profile from the preassessment. It is also dependent on resources, time, the student's preferences for learning, strengths of learning, background or experiences, and especially the objective itself.

Traditionally, processes of learning have been matched to visual, auditory, or kinesthetic learning styles for students. However, these preferred learning styles tend to change with the learning itself, along with the intensity of the challenge perceived. For instance, recently I received a new software program. It was similar to one with which I was already familiar. Therefore, my preference was to open the program and start exploring it rather than read about the program. On the other hand, I also bought a new cell phone recently and had to program it. I had no idea how to do this and was uncomfortable pushing buttons without knowing what I was doing. In this case, my preference was to read about it. That same week, I was involved in a project using a different new piece of technology. I only had to know a little about it, so in this case, rather than being shown the equipment or even touching it, I just asked to be told about it and processed what I needed to know through an auditory mode.

When adjusting the process to meet the needs of different learners, it is important to provide flexibility and multiple options. In many cases, it will take more than one interaction through multiple means of processing for a student to truly comprehend a concept. Adjustments to the learning process are adjustments that provide choice and options for the learner.

Step 8: Determine the flow of classroom activities to include individual, small-group, and whole-group instruction.

In the past, DI was equated with individualized or small-group instruction. It is in fact both of these. It is whole-group instruction as well. The format of the instruction does not determine whether the instruction is differentiated, although it assists in the management of the DI. It is what happens within these formats or settings that determines whether differentiation is truly occurring. After determining the learning processes that students will be pursuing, the teacher must consider the management of the classroom. If there are different activities and configurations, it will be important to determine how classroom order will be maintained.

Whole-Group Instruction

Differentiation can certainly occur within whole-group instruction. This is often accomplished by providing accommodations. Within the whole-group setting, a student or students may be receiving additional supports in order to be successful. Differentiation within this setting often involves providing additional support materials or supports to the environment. Support materials may include electronic translators, visual supports, or graphic organizers. Supports may also include tools such as a calculator or prewritten notes. Supports for whole-group instruction also may involve peer supports as well. Any of these supports are specifically matched to individual students' needs.

SCENARIO

Mrs. Bartels is teaching a math lesson to her whole class. She is teaching the skills of identifying angles, points, and sides on geometric shapes. Before she begins her instruction, she reminds two students that when she says, "Eyes here," that means they need to pay close attention because there is critical information about to be given. She also hands out some manipulatives to some students who need the concrete representations of the geometric shapes. When students are seated, she changes one seat so that one of the more able students is near the two who have limited English skills. This student has been asked to share her work if the two students get lost in the vocabulary of the lesson. Each of these accommodations has been planned, and each is specific to the learner's needs.

Small-Group Instruction

This is most often the format that people think of when they consider DI. Small-group instruction provides one format to allow the instruction to meet different needs. By establishing groups based on a particular commonality, the teacher can work with each small group and focus specifically on what that group needs. It is important to recognize here that small-group instruction is not the same as cooperative learning. Small-group instruction is the practice of grouping students based on strengths and needs or some other pre-assessed commonality and then tailoring the group's work to that. These homogeneous groups are used strategically for instructional purposes (Fisher & Frey, 2001).

Individualized Instruction

While individualized instruction is one aspect of differentiation, it may be the least easily manageable or realistic approach to addressing the varied needs and strengths of students. Classrooms have such great diversity and such a broad spectrum of differences in every aspect that, in most typical classrooms, it would be impossible to tailor all the learning experiences to each student on an individual basis. There are times, however, when individualized instruction is appropriate and reasonable.

In many instances, the individualization occurs during the student's independent work time. This may be in the form of a unique assignment or learning experience, remediation, tutoring, mentoring, or an independent contract. The differentiation that occurs as individualized instruction is generally intensive and short in duration. It often takes on the format of independent work.

Step 9: Determine benchmarks of student performance, and develop tools for ongoing measurement of progress.

After determining the learning process for students along with the classroom format, the next aspect to consider is how achievement will be measured and with what frequency. These measurements are directly related to the planned learning outcome as defined by the standard. The measures, which identify the rate and accuracy of the learning during the learning process, are known as formative assessments (O'Meara, 2010). In many cases, these assessments are done informally throughout the lesson as well as more formally at specific points in the instructional sequence. Informally, these assessments include asking questions or monitoring student performance on a particular skill through observation. They may also include the use of student conferencing, self-assessments, or peer reviews (Fisher & Frey, 2001). Providing short independent practice opportunities that are recorded or assessed using a checklist, rubric, or graph of progress is a strategy to measure and monitor growth. These frequent assessments can be easily implemented and managed through the use of technology, response cards, or electronic response systems. No matter which strategy is used for the assessment or response, the purpose is to gain information regarding how the student is learning in relation to the desired outcome or objective. These measures must be planned and deliberate in order to provide direction for instruction and supports.

Step 10: Develop criteria for the summative product or performance that accurately reflect the intended outcomes of the unit.

It is important to determine how mastery will be assessed at the end of the experience. This is the summative assessment. It is designed to provide an opportunity for a student to communicate what he or she has learned. The design must be directly aligned to the intended outcome and objectives. Whether it is a test, product, or performance, it is critical that criteria are established to clearly identify the expectations and definition of mastery. These criteria should be communicated to the students before ever approaching this assessment.

All of these steps of planning and preparation are required in order to effectively and systematically differentiate instruction. Each element builds on the other and creates a student-centered focus. It is this process that prepares a teacher to provide the responsive instruction that matches students' strengths and needs to their learning experiences.

SUMMARY

DI is a systematic process of both planning and delivery. It focuses on the student and his or her relationship to the content. It requires knowledge of the students and the ability to respond to that information. The purpose of

DI is to ensure success for all learners by providing the systematic, effective supports and challenges needed for each student to reach his or her highest potential. There are specific steps in designing, planning, and implementing DI, each of which is intended to prepare and provide an environment and opportunity for honoring the diverse student populations in our schools. The steps begin with examining the standards and distinguishing between the facts and skills and conceptual understandings. The steps involve designing assessments to determine progress as well as mastery.

QUESTIONS TO CONSIDER

- Which steps of the instructional planning process do you practice most often? Which do you tend to overlook? What evidence do you have showing that you implement any or all of these steps?
- Which of these steps do you find to be the most critical to plan before implementing a lesson?
- How much emphasis do you place on the planning and preparation in order to be responsive to students?
- When do you find time to plan and/or collaborate? Are there other options?
- How does your classroom instruction reflect the honoring of student differences?
- Do you offer different approaches to the content by providing various materials or different avenues?
- Do you provide different learning processing opportunities? How do you manage these in your classroom?
- What resources do you use to be sure your content information is current and accurate?
- What resources within your school provide supports for your efforts? What do you think you need the most in order to better implement differentiated instruction?

3

The Merging of DI and RTI

It was once thought by some that children of color would somehow taint the classrooms with their presence. Imagine the emptiness we would have in our classrooms today without the gifts these students bring. Together our children create such a richer environment. Just as our students do, together RTI and differentiation of instruction also provide a richer environment for our classrooms.

HOW DO THEY FIT TOGETHER?

The term *differentiated instruction* (DI), along with the related professional development, has been around for more than 50 years now. It is a common term in education and is included in just about every educational conference, publication, or webcast that deals with instruction and curriculum. Yet despite the amount of time and attention DI has received, the implementation of the practice still falls into a sketchy area. How is it actually implemented and managed in the classroom? What does it look like? How is its effectiveness measured? There is still a certain degree of vagueness to the topic in many arenas.

Now DI shares the limelight with Response to Intervention/Instruction (RTI). It is clear that RTI will change the way we educate students and the way the educational system functions. However, RTI is relatively new and there are a tremendous number of unanswered questions and uncharted water still to be resolved in many areas. Across the United States, many education departments are trying to comprehend the principles of RTI, implement practices, and personalize the model by assimilating it into existing structures. One structure that lends itself to helping to make sense of RTI is DI.

Commonalities and Rationale for the Marriage

There are several reasons these two philosophies and functioning frameworks fit together (see Figure 3.1). The most obvious is that they are both married to the practices of curriculum and instruction, which also include behavior and classroom management. Both DI and RTI address important aspects of teaching that need to be a focus in order for effective learning to take place. Another reason is that they both take into account outside factors and influences. Both acknowledge that learning does not occur in a vacuum and that a classroom is not a completely predictable setting. A related common consideration is the focus on environmental factors as well as the learner, the material, and the instruction. Finally, and most important, both DI and RTI put students at the center of the practice. Decisions are made based on students rather than on a book, tradition, or certain rules of practice. The practices are responsive to the learners.

Figure 3.1   Foundations of Differentiated Instruction and Response to Intervention/Instruction

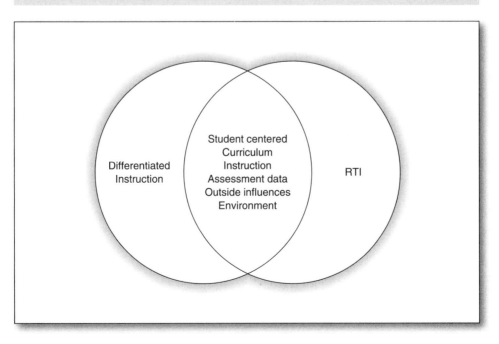

The following are specific principles critical to both DI and RTI:

- Assessment results drive instruction.
- Flexible timing and grouping are hallmarks.
- Established standards and expectations are critical.
- The frameworks are systematic and intentional.
- Opportunity for success is assured.
- The Individuals with Disabilities Education and Improvement Act (IDEIA) and No Child Left Behind (NCLB) provide legislative support and strength.

Assessment results drive instruction.

In both practices, decisions are made based on student performance as indicated by assessments. DI calls for pre-assessments to be implemented to determine levels of understanding, interests, work habits and styles, background experiences, or any number of other aspects that impact students' understanding or learning of the content. The information from the pre-assessment is then used to design the learning activities and instructional experiences carried out in the classroom. It is also used to determine the level of support needed for student success. In the case of RTI, there is a strong emphasis on data-driven decision making. RTI requires collecting data to measure student progress or mastery. RTI begins and ends with data collection. By examining data, RTI provides the framework for supports and learning experiences based on the results of the data.

Flexible timing and grouping are hallmarks.

In DI, learning experiences are planned systematically and intentionally. However, DI also acknowledges that there are circumstances beyond a teacher's control and even the best of plans sometimes don't fit the time or need. DI allows for adjustments to be made in response to the learner's state, environmental factors, or any other element that impacts learning. Like RTI, DI provides supports for students only when needed and not all the time for all experiences. Both practices require flexible grouping so that each student is participating in learning that is challenging but not too frustrating. RTI is also designed to allow for supports when needed. It consists of measures used to determine the effectiveness of the supports along with the intensity and duration in which the supports are needed.

Established standards and expectations are critical.

The process of DI begins by examining standards to determine the desired learning outcomes. Pre-assessment is then administered to determine the relationship between the learner and those outcomes. Without establishing standards and knowing clearly what the intended outcome is, DI can easily become random acts of teaching. A destination is required in order to create a route to go somewhere; without clearly established outcomes, instruction and related practices are unclear and unfocused.

RTI also clearly requires standards and expectations. The RTI process not only establishes the intended outcome but also measures the increments of progress that students need in order to meet that outcome within the designated time frame. Initial student assessment establishes a starting point, and then assessments along the way measure the rate of learning that is occurring to reach that outcome. These assessments reflecting the rate of progress are used to determine the amount of supports and services needed to help the student maintain progress to meet the outcome in a timely fashion.

The frameworks are systematic and intentional.

DI involves a specific process by which to plan, assess, instruct, and provide supports to learners. Each of these steps is critical and equally important. Ignoring any one of the steps creates a platform for ineffective learning opportunities. DI provides a decision-making framework in which to determine teaching strategies, learning activities, grouping formats, types of assessments, and modes and styles of the learning as well as communicating the results of learning. RTI takes this systematic process a step further. The tiers are established with the intent that a tier of more intensity is designed to support the learner in being successful with the tier of less support. For instance, Tier 2 is designed to support learning at Tier 1, and Tier 3 is designed to support learning at Tier 2. Rather than providing random learning supports for students who need additional supports or services, the learning is seamless and the desired outcome is the same for all supports and services for an individual.

Opportunity for success is assured.

One of the strongest arguments for implementing DI and RTI is the shared philosophy that no child should ever fall through the cracks. In fact, rather than waiting for a student to approach the crack, early efforts are made to avoid any possibility of that happening. Both of these initiatives focus on successful learning experiences for all students. By identifying each student's present level along with needs for supports and services in order to achieve the desired learning outcomes, teachers can give each child the instruction and learning opportunities needed. Each student is met at his or her current level and then provided with the supports needed to make gains. With the data collection required of RTI, there should be no student left unnoticed and no needs left unaddressed.

IDEIA and NCLB provide legislative support and strength.

IDEIA and NCLB support these processes with the renewed focus on highest achievement for all students. The legislation uses the general education expectations as the foundation of expectations for all students, including those who receive special education services as well as those receiving only general education services. IDEIA emphasizes providing supports and services within the general education setting using quality curriculum rather than labeling a student and removing him or her from the setting. It sets an expectation for student success in general education through pooling resources to meet student needs. These resources are the supports and services of both DI and RTI. Further, NCLB strengthens these efforts with an emphasis on the highest student achievement with measures of accountability. With this legislation, the educational system is required to be accountable for the success of all students at all ability and need levels. Again, this emphasizes general education as the baseline for expectations of all students, including those identified as having special needs.

DIFFERENCES BETWEEN DI AND RTI

Although there are some striking commonalities between these two educational processes, there are also some ways in which they are different (see Figure 3.2). The differences include the following:

- foundations and uniformity
- instructional options available
- student population emphasis
- emphasis on quantifiable data

Foundations and Uniformity

There are differences in the levels of consistency and uniformity between these two processes. DI grew as a best practice in the field of education over an extended period of time. It came into its own through quality research and professional development in the interest of providing the best instruction to students. *Differentiation* became a term used across all disciplines in education. By the broad use of the practice, educators have several definitions and countless opportunities to learn varied perspectives of DI. Some of the language is common due to strong leaders in the field of professional development. However, the practices and descriptors may be vastly different across the large scope of education.

RTI on the other hand has come into the field of education with consistency and a uniform voice that DI did not have. RTI has specifically defined a process for problem solving, expectations for the core instruction, and

Figure 3.2   Differences Between Differentiated Instruction and Response to Intervention

	DI	RTI
Uniformity	Decisions based on best practices and teacher decision making	Decisions based on protocols and only research and evidence-based practices
Instructional options	Inclusive of all disciplines; takes into account learning modalities and preferences, and allows for student choice	Focus on reading, mathematics, and behavior; systematic process for responding to student performance
Student population focus	General education classroom is initial stage, designed for all students regardless of performance or ability	Close ties to special education; designed for learners who need more than what is provided in the general curriculum
Use of data	Formative assessments and progress monitoring encouraged as a best practice	Data drives decision making; protocols are in place for data collection and interpretation

processes of assessment and data collection. While the processes and practices vary across the United States, the framework remains relatively consistent with three to four tiers. The National Center on Response to Intervention has standard protocols for interventions, and there is an effort to have a common understanding of the tiers. RTI defines research and evidence-based practices as required. Because DI came about as a grassroots, need-based effort, these protocols and standards were not set into place.

Instructional Options Available

Along with the established protocols and frameworks of RTI come parameters for instructional practices that are not present in DI. RTI focuses efforts on highest student achievement in the areas of academics, specifically reading and mathematics, and also behavior. Therefore, responses relate to data collected in those areas of student performance. While DI is also centered on highest student achievement, it is less limited in the scope of instructional responses. Differentiation takes into account information from assessments on student interests and motivations as well as academic and behavioral performance. DI is all-inclusive of disciplines and is open to every aspect of the whole student. Differentiation in social studies is as important as it is in language arts or physical education.

The basis for decision making may or may not be based on specific academic performance on an assessment. Providing student choice is a powerful aspect of DI.

These differences are a result of the nature of these two processes. RTI has strong foundations in systematic decision making based on academic data, and DI has an element of flexibility as one if its hallmarks. Both are valuable for the strengths they offer, and both are necessary in order to provide the best educational opportunities for students.

Student Population Emphasis

The movement toward implementing DI was largely a result of the efforts of educators to meet the needs of all students in the classroom. It was recognized that the student population was diverse, and getting more and more so almost daily. General education teachers were seeking new practices and strategies to meet the needs of students. DI and its related practices rose to meet those needs. It provides guidance for teachers to honor the diversity and strive toward highest student achievement for all students in the classroom. It includes students who are performing well above the mean, who learn in different ways, or who need additional supports or accommodations to be successful. For the most part, DI was most needed and adopted by teachers in general education classrooms. It provided them with multiple strategies for assessing, grouping, instructing, and evaluating students.

RTI includes the word *intervention* in its name, which suggests a focus on struggling learners. While RTI is a process for all students, the emphasis is on students who are not meeting the general education expectations. It does not apply to all students across the board in the same way. A student who is performing well and meeting expectations would not be served through all the configurations or levels of RTI. Tiers 2 and 3 are designed for those students whose needs are not being met through instruction within the core curriculum. There are still many unanswered questions regarding how RTI applies to highly advanced students whose needs are not being met through the core curriculum. While DI provided in Tier 1 meets the needs of many students, there are still others on both ends of the spectrum who have needs that go beyond the core curriculum. Only in some cases are the students on the high end being considered for Tier 2 or 3 services and supports.

Emphasis on Quantifiable Data

DI is rooted in the concept of pre-assessment as a decision-making tool. It guides initial decisions regarding instruction. DI also strongly emphasizes formative assessment and progress monitoring as ways to determine the effectiveness of the learning experience. These assessments are part of the best practices included in the implementation of DI.

RTI has a strong emphasis on assessment and progress monitoring. In fact, this is a hallmark of RTI. Data are collected frequently and routinely for the purpose of identifying the student's response to the instruction and learning experience. With RTI, specific criteria are established. Standard protocols determine the type of data collected, the assessment tools used to collect the data, and methods for interpreting the data in order to make instructional decisions. RTI formalizes the processes of progress monitoring and provides guidance as to appropriate responses to the findings.

CHALLENGES

With all these commonalities and ways the two fit so nicely together, why is it such a challenge to implement RTI with DI and answer questions regarding implementation?

First of all, there is a challenge presented in understanding what RTI is and how it functions. In some instances, this has been the result of a lack of a preplanned professional development rollout. In many cases, teachers and administrators are building the plane as they fly it when it comes to RTI. The pace of RTI coming on the scene has been more rapid than the educational system is accustomed to and has taken some educators by storm. Each year additional responsibilities, challenges, and new initiatives overwhelm educators, and RTI may contribute to that feeling if it is not clear what it is and how it is to be implemented.

One of the significant outcomes of the implementation of RTI is how it affects the identification of students for special needs programs. RTI practices move in a direction of meeting the needs of students as soon as the needs are recognized. RTI is an early-response system. This is in opposition to the practice of recognizing a need and then focusing efforts on identifying a disability so that the student can receive the services needed through the special education system. In this model of the past, a student became identified as having a special need and then became the responsibility of the special education teacher to "fix," which, research tells us, the teacher is often unsuccessful in doing. The National Center on Secondary Education and Transition found that the graduation rate for students with special needs in the United States is only 57% (Leuchovius, 2006). One reason for this lack of success at graduation may be due to the fact that access to the rigorous general education curriculum and instruction often end when special education services begin. Practices include slowing the pace and diluting the rigor. With RTI, there is no end to the access to the rigors of general education. With this shift, less attention is paid to the processes of qualifying a student for special needs services and more attention is paid to what a student needs in order to experience success. This shift creates two major challenges as changes are taking place.

The first is that the de-emphasis on the identification of students with disabilities creates a smaller number of students identified for programs for students with special needs. These programs are attached to both state and national funding models. As schools implement RTI and identify fewer students for programs, the schools' funding may be reduced. The RTI initiative and the funding systems need to merge so that educational institutions are not penalized for implementing RTI and identifying fewer students for special needs programs.

The second challenge is not as significant to the system but often creates frustration among educators. A key stakeholder in the identification of students for special education programs is the psychologist. In the past, this person has held the key to the services-and-support door. If a student was determined eligible as a result of testing, the student was given an individualized education program (IEP) and a plan was set to provide the needed service or supports. With RTI, psychologists have become heavily involved in implementation as they recognize the change in their role. This group, in many instances, has taken the initiative head-on and has become active in the leadership of the RTI movement. Their expertise with data interpretation provides a strong asset to the RTI efforts.

However, this strong activism by school psychologists has been left unmatched by other educational divisions in many places. Reading initiatives and DI still hold the headlines in professional educators' circles. Educators focus on instructional methods and practices related to RTI while the psychologists focus more on procedural protocols and evaluation. The imbalance and lack of a unified voice has created problems that lead to some of the confusion that exists today. Due to the targeted expertise and awareness in the field of psychology, many leaders have created a focus of RTI, which has placed evaluation and program protocol in the spotlight. Problem solving and data collection related to these two areas have become central to the RTI conversations. This is reinforced by IDEIA and related reports, which caution the over-identification of certain populations in special needs programs. This would not be a problem if the instructional methods and interventions were given the same amount of attention. However, educators in the classroom are trying to stay above water by remaining focused on instructional methods, strategies, and accountability.

Due to this imbalance, the rollout of RTI in many places began with the problem-solving team and a focus on new or different processes and procedures for students to become eligible for special needs programs. For the general education classroom teacher, much of this conversation was removed from the day-to-day practices in the classroom. Teachers were hearing about RTI but not as part of teaching and instructional practices. This is in no way faulting the leaders in the field of psychology who have focused on the aspects of RTI with which they were most familiar and those that impacted them directly. However, this resulted in teachers not being able to make connections between RTI and daily classroom practices.

Another by-product that has resulted from the psychologists being in the lead of the RTI movement is the emphasis on the processes and protocols of problem solving in isolation. These topics, presented before discussions of classroom practices related to instruction, have made teachers and instructional practices seem outside the RTI framework. RTI in its biggest picture starts with Tier 1 and the core curriculum. It is only when a student needs more supports and services that Tier 2 or Tier 3 is considered along with specialized supports, services, and/or evaluations. With that comes the possibility for eligibility determinations for special programs. These considerations are made after several other instructional practices and interventions are implemented. Presenting RTI by starting with a focus on evaluation and eligibility is like teaching the alphabet starting with the letter *M*. There are many practices that come before that point in the RTI framework and many that come after. Starting in the middle makes seeing the whole picture much more difficult.

Another hindrance resulting from the focus being on evaluation and eligibility is the misconception that the purpose of RTI is to reduce services for students or reduce the numbers of students determined to be eligible for special needs programs. RTI does, in fact, affect those outcomes. It actually increases, rather than reduces, services and accessibility to services for students. This is accomplished by recognizing that a student needs additional supports or services and by providing for that need without having to first assign the student a label. All students have access to additional supports and services as needed, not just the ones who have been determined eligible for services. Because these supports and services are in place, there is less need to determine eligibility for a program and label a student as having a special need or disability. This is a result of RTI, not a cause.

A final significant challenge comes with the balance between what has been common practice and what needs to change. Many aspects of RTI are practices that have been part of best teaching practices for years. In some ways, it is easy to claim that RTI is nothing new or different. Yet, it does present the need for a paradigm shift in the way educators think about student learning and interventions. It has been common practice to identify a student struggling to learn and send that student to someone who can "help." This sees the problem as the student learning rather than the instruction. It reinforces the notion that the teacher does not need to adjust instruction but rather find a different teacher or interventionist for the student. This diminishes the demand for DI. Yet, in fact, RTI demands more DI rather than less. The first step after identifying a student in need of additional support is to adjust the instruction through differentiation. It is easy to overlook that essential component unless there is a change in the way we think about interventions. They start with differentiating classroom instruction rather than with finding another educator to provide supplemental supports or interventions.

CURRICULUM AND ASSESSMENT, INSTRUCTION, AND THE ENVIRONMENT

Despite the challenges and differences between RTI and DI, both have a place in the exemplary classroom. This is because their relationship and that of the related factors to each other and to curriculum, assessment, instruction, and the learning environment create the stage on which the student becomes the focus. Each of these elements affects individual students differently. Both DI and RTI acknowledge these as elements that can be influenced for the purpose of improving the opportunities for student success. While a universal core curriculum is established for RTI, DI reminds us that each student has a different experience, background, and level of understanding with the material. Together, RTI and DI work hand in hand to create a systematic and structured framework of curricula with the flexibility to respond to each learner's needs. RTI and DI both approach instruction and the environment with the understanding that different learners will need varying levels of support.

The Curriculum and Assessment

Often, these two elements of the instructional process are viewed as two completely different components. While that is, in fact, often the case, here they are addressed as one to emphasize the commonalities of the two as well as the dependence of assessment on the curriculum. Assessment is essentially the by-product of the interactions the learner has with the curriculum, instruction, and environment (see Figure 3.3). Therefore, it is placed with the curriculum because they both follow the same principles within the RTI and DI frameworks.

In both RTI and DI, it is essential to start with a systematic, research-based, quality curriculum. The curriculum provides the structure and can be viewed as similar to the support structures and beams of a building. It is critical that it has been well planned, carefully designed, and constantly monitored. The curriculum is designed with high expectations for all

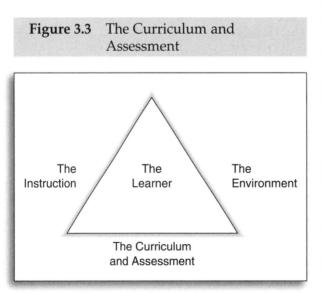

Figure 3.3 The Curriculum and Assessment

The Instruction

The Learner

The Environment

The Curriculum and Assessment

students along with expectations of success for all students. It is developed with the intent that all students will achieve success with the standards. Curriculum does not refer to a program or textbook. Instead it refers to the standards and learning objectives that have been systematically mapped out and selected as intentional learning opportunities. In language involving curriculum, RTI names this the *core curriculum.* It is important to have a solid framework on which to function. RTI needs a strong core curriculum on which to base instructional decisions and by which to measure student progress. DI needs this strong core in order to implement varying levels of supports and accommodations within the core curriculum.

Both RTI and DI depend on clear, measurable outcomes as well. These expected outcomes or assessment measures must be consistent as well as systematic. There is one defined expectation for all learners that has been clearly targeted throughout the instructional and learning process. This target is consistent for all students, and the expectation remains the same. RTI and DI both respond to each learner by providing accommodations or supports to the way the learner will achieve and model the desired outcome.

The Instruction

A second component of the learning process for students is the instruction provided. Instructional approaches are expected to be systematic and matched to both the curriculum content and the strengths and needs of the learner. The phrase *implemented with fidelity* has come to be used frequently when discussing instruction. This refers to the instruction as well as instructional methods selected. Again, these are research-based practices matched to the students. Within both RTI and DI, this emphasis on quality and fidelity is essential. Fidelity is defined as the degree to which instruction follows the intent and design of the strategy or program according to research findings (National Association of State Directors of Special Education, 2006). Both DI and RTI strongly emphasize the need to move away from instructional methods chosen without rationale or matched to the learner outcome. Instruction must be based on evidence or research as reflected by student success. There must be data to support the use of an instructional strategy if it is to be implemented. When implemented, it is critical that there be monitoring on the fidelity of the implementation—not as a check for teacher competency, but as a way to monitor the match between the implementation and the data or research that supports the instructional practice.

A second reason for the emphasis on fidelity is that instruction is expected to be responsive to individual student strengths and needs. Both RTI and DI acknowledge that a one-size-fits-all model will not work. Therefore, adjustments and adaptations must be made in order to meet the needs of students. In making these adjustments, it is important not to move away from what the research has proved to be effective.

RTI and DI both focus on instruction as a way to provide opportunities for student success. Both include the term *instruction* within their own names. Both are founded on the idea that instruction must be responsive and dynamic. Instruction is the dance between the learner and the content. It includes the amounts of supports and the amount of independence a learner receives in order to be successful. Both RTI and DI put those supports at the forefront of the processes, with high expectations for student success as the goal.

The Environment

Like instruction, the environment may also require varying levels of supports and independent opportunities for a learner to be successful. The environment affects the learning process as well as the motivational, social, emotional, and behavioral aspects. RTI and DI recognize that the environment plays a significant role in the learning process. Both encourage a fostering, consistent, motivating environment to be provided, an environment in which success is a frequent experience.

RTI emphasizes consistency within the environment. RTI supports schoolwide behavior plans in which all students have the same expectations and have a clear understanding of those expectations. Teachers use common language, and acceptable and unacceptable behaviors are consistent across classrooms within a school. These expectations are established and are clear to students, with the intent and expectation that they will be able to be successful in meeting these expectations.

Where DI and RTI are the same in relation to the environment is in their practice of acknowledging a student's response to the environment and expectations. It is expected that the structure be firmly in place and the same for all students. However, it is also expected that different students will need different levels of support in achieving success. These supports are provided as a response to student performance.

For both the instructional and environmental components, we can see a cyclical effect within the system (see Figure 3.4). Clear expectations are established. Students respond to the expectations at varying levels of performance and success, and then educators respond to those student responses with varying levels of supports and services. The supports and services provided as a response to student needs are one element of DI. Then the educator assesses the student's performance with the supports to determine the effectiveness of the supports in helping the student achieve the learning goal. The assessment of the student performance determines the actions of the educator. The actions of the educator impact student performance.

Figure 3.4 The Cycle of Expectations

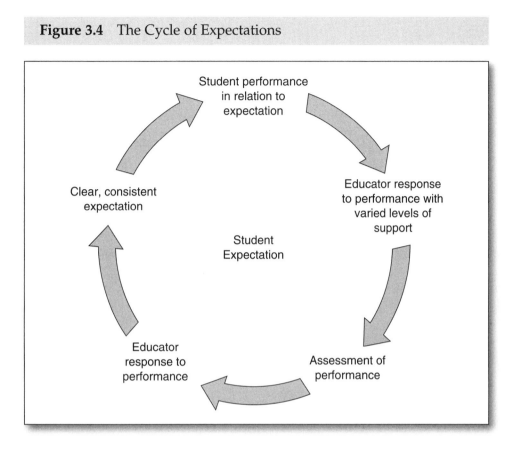

Student performance
in relation to
expectation

Educator response
to performance with
varied levels of
support

Clear, consistent
expectation

Student
Expectation

Educator
response to
performance

Assessment of
performance

SCENARIO

The school rule at Muldoon Elementary School states that all students will walk in the hallways. Students clearly understand that this rule includes not skipping, hopping, leaping, or jogging. There have been several discussions about this rule and its need due to safety issues. Muldoon Elementary is a Positive Behavioral Support school where expectations are clear and all educators enforce and reward behaviors consistently.

Mrs. Clark notices that, at the end of each day, there is a group of fourth-grade students who always run down the hall. Each day she yells as they run by, ordering them to walk. One day, right at the end of the school day, she stops these students and asks why they cannot seem to follow this rule. Her concern is not only the violation of the rule but also that they run through the kindergarten hallway and are much larger than the younger students. The older students run and jump around the little ones, putting them in danger. The fourth-grade students explain that they are running to the bus to get the back seats before

(Continued)

(Continued)

the fifth graders. They claim they want the back seats so that the fifth graders won't throw things at them from behind. Mrs. Clark is not sure if that is actually true or if they want to sit in the back seats just because it is cool at that age. Either way, Mrs. Clark now understands the issue and can react to the problem to stop these behaviors.

Mrs. Clark speaks to the bus driver, who easily agrees that assigned seats would make her life easier as well. Mrs. Clark and the bus driver determine that the fourth graders will be allowed in the back seats one week and the fifth graders the following week. This rotation will remain unless there is an incident with throwing anything on the bus. In that case, the group of students who threw objects would be made to sit at the front for two consecutive weeks. The students agree that this plan is acceptable and agree to comply.

For the next three weeks, Mrs. Clark monitors the running activity in the hallway. She checks daily and finds that the students who ride that particular bus are no longer running in the hallway. In fact, because they are not in such a rush, a few of the older students are stopping to walk to the bus with younger siblings or neighbors. She provides the students who are now walking appropriately with reinforcements for their positive behaviors.

In a more academic-based situation, Mrs. Clark also uses RTI frameworks and differentiates her instruction within her classroom. She was teaching her kindergarten students about volume and surface area. She used different containers to teach volume and discussed how different-shaped containers could hold the same amount of a liquid. She had four containers that all held one liter, yet the four containers were different in appearance. Although all the containers were cylinders, each had a different diameter. Therefore, the taller, slender one had the same volume as a lower, wider one. Mrs. Clark extended the lesson to help students discover that the amount of space each container needed on a table was different. She had students create a chart that reflected all containers that held one liter, then the students ordered the containers based on the surface area they needed on the table.

Mrs. Clark noticed during this lesson, through targeted questioning as a formative assessment, that three students seemed lost, not understanding the concept. They could not grasp that when the shape changed, the volume did not. They seemed to believe that the tallest container would hold the most and the shortest container the least. Mrs. Clark brought these students to the sink, where they were able to pour water into the containers and witness that each container held the same amount of water. She had them trace the bottoms of each of the containers on paper and cut them out in order to visually see the differences. When the students all shared their charts and discoveries, these students were able to match their cutouts to each of the containers on the classroom chart. Mrs. Clark gave all of the students a short summative assessment designed to reflect their understandings after the lesson was complete. The students who used the manipulatives and water reflected an accurate conceptual understanding, as did the others in the classroom.

In these scenarios, the expectations and objectives were made clear. Students responded to the expectations in a way that reflected the need for a change to help encourage more appropriate behaviors or more academic supports. This was determined by evidence of their behaviors and performance. Mrs. Clark differentiated her approaches to students as a response to their performances. She did not try to implement a new policy or practice for all students on all buses. She did not create a different lesson for some students. Instead she adjusted the conditions to help students achieve her desired performance and understanding. These efforts were targeted toward the students in need of changes in behavior or supports, not all students. The expectations for the students did not change. The support, in the form of a seating plan or concrete manipulatives, was in direct response to student performance. Finally, after taking action, Mrs. Clark followed through with data collection and assessment to see whether the approaches were successful.

SUMMARY

DI and RTI are processes that are necessary for all students to experience success and achieve at the highest possible levels. While the two share some strong characteristics, there are also significant ways in which they are different. These differences reinforce and strengthen each other in many ways to create a classroom with the highest opportunities for success. The most valuable attribute of these two processes is that both put the student at the forefront and center of all decision making and provide multiple supports, services, and opportunities for success for all learners.

QUESTIONS TO CONSIDER

- What degree of implementation of DI is evident in your classroom? What evidence do you have to reflect that?
- What supports does the RTI system at your school offer you to better meet the needs of your students?
- What collaboration is occurring to best support efforts to implement both DI and RTI?
- What misconceptions do you witness regarding DI and RTI?
- How do you see the two processes together meeting the needs of all students in your classroom? Think of specific students.

PART II

Tier 1 RTI With Differentiated Instruction

Practical Application in the Classroom

4

Tier 1—Curriculum and Instruction

Strong, research-based programs are essential—but so is strong, quality instruction. Neither stands on its own.

QUALITY CORE CURRICULUM

One of the major premises of Response to Instruction/Intervention (RTI) is the need for a quality core curriculum to be solidly in place. One of the foundational principles of differentiated instruction (DI) is that the process starts with the standards. Both practices expect the curriculum to have a leading role in effectively meeting students' needs. It is less important which curriculum is used and more important that it has been developed with elements of systematic progression, grade-appropriate expectations, and clear, measureable outcomes. In both practices, reflection back onto the standards is essential. Many commercial programs and textbooks will provide resources to address the curriculum, but it is important to remember that the programs and materials used are the tools, and not the curriculum itself.

There are many commercial programs that are advertised as research-based systems of curriculum and tools to help provide quality instruction. These should be considered with caution and investigated. The What Works Clearinghouse (www.ies.ed.gov/ncee/wwc), initiated by the

U.S. Department of Education's Institute of Education Sciences, is a trusted source of research-based evidence of effective practices and programs.

In most cases, the teacher has little control over selecting a curriculum and sometimes the programs used to address the curriculum. The decisions related to the development of curriculum standards are generally left to the leaders in the school district or departments at the state level. However, the teacher does have control over the amount of attention placed on ensuring that the core curriculum really is one of high quality. There are elements of quality to consider when evaluating a curriculum and elements that can be altered to enhance a curriculum. Most important, the aspect of having clearly stated, measureable outcomes not only is within the teacher's control, but is necessary for the implementation of differentiation and RTI.

SCENARIO

Mrs. White has been hired to teach third grade. She has spent time studying the district and state standards so that she will be prepared to start her job. She does not know what tools, programs, textbooks, or other resources will be available to her, but she understands that clarity of the standards must come first. She finds that each content area has different levels of specificity with the standards. Here are some of the standards she finds in three content areas:

Language Arts

- Use self-correction to re-read after recognizing text that does not make sense
- Apply sound-letter knowledge to decode unknown words quickly and accurately in context
- Use context clues to determine meanings of unfamiliar words
- Identify a text's features (title, subheadings, captions, illustrations), use them to make and confirm predictions, and establish a purpose for reading
- Recognize that author's voice affects the narrative in tone and message

Mathematics

- Identify, describe, and apply division and multiplication as inverse operations
- Compare and order fractions, including fractions greater than 1
- Solve nonroutine problems by making a table, chart, or list
- Tell time to the nearest minute and determine how much time has elapsed between two given times

Science

- Explain that stars can be different in size and brightness yet all except the Sun look like points of light

(Continued)

(Continued)

- Recognize that the Sun appears larger because it is the closest star to the Earth
- Identify that the Sun is a star that emits energy
- Demonstrate that radiant energy from the Sun can heat objects

Mrs. White begins by identifying which of these should be a focus for instruction and which should be learned as independent tasks. She does this by examining which standards and objectives are simply a matter of learned skills and facts and which have the depth to lead to conceptual understandings. She quickly sees that several of the language arts standards require several sets of subskills to achieve the standard. For instance, the standard related to decoding involves many phonics skills. These skills will require more independent practice and a great deal of repetition. She thinks about how she can provide independent practice using computer software programs, homework practice, centers, and other independent learning opportunities. Mrs. White makes a note to herself to focus her resources in language arts on acquiring centers and software programs that will provide quality opportunities to practice the skills involved with the standards related to phonics. There will be less instruction required for those standards because they are skills, and after initial instruction these require accurate practice rather than multiple, new learning experiences. She knows there will be some students who struggle with the phonics skills and will need additional supports. She will provide accommodations for those students as they learn, but overall, the instruction will focus less on these skills and more on the conceptual standards.

Mrs. White identifies the language arts standard requiring students to recognize the influence of author's voice as one that involves conceptual understandings as well as the skills. While she will provide opportunities for students to practice the discrete skill of identifying author's voice, she will focus her instruction on how an author manipulates a story through personal point of view and tone. The instruction here will go beyond the skills so that students develop an awareness that authors write with a purpose and that tone and mood are developed by the writer. Mrs. White also sees this standard directly relating to writing and other content areas. She highlights this standard to embed in other content areas as well. By looking at the language arts standards, she identifies skills that need some quality, clear instruction and a great deal of practice. She also recognizes one standard that addresses conceptual understandings rather than just skills. This will become a main area of focus for her instruction.

Having identified a conceptual standard, there are new issues that must be addressed. For the standards that involve identifying letters and their relationships to specific sounds, there is clearly a defined degree of mastery that is implicit. Each of those skill-based standards is measureable and easy to assess. Through quizzes or demonstrations, students can show their ability to identify the sound-letter relationship. However, standards that involve conceptual understandings are more ambiguous. Mrs. White has to determine how she will measure student recognition of author's voice and its impact on text.

She has to develop her own expectations, levels of mastery, and quality in order to determine whether students have met this standard.

Mrs. White next looks at the mathematics standards and has many questions about them. She sees these standards as important skills but wonders about their depth and breadth. She asks herself, "How many fractions must be compared and ordered? What is considered a nonroutine problem?" For all of these standards she also wonders, "What degree of accuracy do the students need in order to be considered proficient?" She decides that one of the first conversations she needs to have is with the school math coach and the grade-level teachers.

Mrs. White is clear that the first unit in science will center on a study of the Sun and stars. She sees these standards as related but feels they need to be brought together under a big idea of some kind. She decides that the standards really involve the understanding of a deeper concept. She thinks about teaching the unit through the lens of a big idea, stating, "Perspective is sometimes deceiving."

For each content area, Mrs. White examines and dissects each of the standards for third grade. The more she works with the standards, the clearer she becomes on where her instructional focus will be, what areas need to be developed through centers and independent work, and where her questions are. She is glad she has a whole month before starting her year of teaching!

What Mrs. White is doing takes a great deal of time and thought. It is best done in teams of educators who all work with the same standards. In many cases, standards can have many different interpretations and levels of expectations. Without explicitly defined outcomes, there is no clear level of mastery with which to hold students accountable. There is no way to separate proficient from less-than-proficient performance when the outcome is vague. It is impossible to collect data when there is no target. Without a target, there is no way to determine how close or far a student is from the bull's eye. Without this information gleaned from examining the standards, differentiating instruction and learning is merely an exercise in providing random supports or challenges with no intention. Therefore, it is critical to examine the standards or desired learning outcomes closely and thoroughly. Each desired outcome must be clear and measureable for it to be defined as part of the quality core curriculum.

What to Do

Within the curriculum, examine the standards or desired learning outcomes. Look at each and ask these questions:

- Do I know exactly what the standard is asking of the student?
- Can I accurately determine whether a student can or cannot master that standard?
- Can I determine how far or close a student is to mastering the standard?

These questions should be able to be answered for any standard that is based on acquiring facts and skills. For any standard or desired outcome that cannot be answered in the affirmative for all three questions, first think about the desired learning outcome. What does it really look like? Complete this sentence:

"If a student mastered this standard at a specific grade level, he or she would be able to _____."

Then answer these questions with that response in mind:

- How can I think about the standard in a way that makes it clear what is expected?
- How can I add criteria in order for it to become measurable?

The conceptual standards will often require these questions to be answered. Conceptual standards are often ones that will apply to multiple grade levels at different levels of depth or complexity. For instance, understanding how an author can influence the reader through word choice is a standard that could be appropriate at many different levels. At third grade the criteria and expectations would be different than at ninth grade. However, these standards that deal with meaningful, conceptual understanding are the ones that should be given this additional attention and discussion.

QUALITY BEHAVIOR PLAN

Just as they require a quality core curriculum, DI and RTI also require the implementation of a quality core behavior plan. This is needed for the same reasons as the quality core curriculum. A behavior plan must be clear in its expectations of students and contain required elements that can be assessed and measured. A quality behavior plan may be part of a school-wide plan, or it may be unique to each classroom. Ideally, behavior plans are the same across settings so that students are clear about what is expected of them. This is only the case, however, when the behavior plan itself is clear and specific. Otherwise, left to interpretation, a schoolwide behavior plan is interpreted in countless ways, and students do not experience the necessary consistency.

In establishing a quality behavior plan, the same steps apply as in the curriculum. The first step is to determine the desired outcome. What behaviors are desired? Too often, in the name of saving time, teachers post a list of classroom rules, read them to students, and expect students to be clear on the expectations. In many cases, they are rules such as "Be respectful." What exactly does that look like? If a group of teachers were asked that question, the answers could likely be quite different for each teacher. Therefore, it is important to take the time to define exactly what the desired behaviors are. For instance, instead of a classroom rule that says "No talking when someone else is talking," a clearer one is "Only one person speaks at a time. If someone is speaking, wait until the person is done before speaking." This makes it possible for students to clearly understand what is expected. It is also easily measured. A person can observe a particular student and determine how frequently the student does or does not follow the stated expectation.

Because each element of a quality behavior plan is like the curricular expectations, these too should be stated as desired behavior in positive terms. Rather than "The student will not run in the hallway," the desired performance is stated as "The student will walk in the hallway." The concept of targeting the desired outcome is particularly important with regard to behavior. In the hallway example, if the standard is focused on what a student should not do—in this case, run down the hallway—then anything else may be acceptable. That means skipping, hopping, or leaping would all be acceptable. Hopefully, the students will opt for walking. With behavior, there are plenty of options of what would be acceptable if the objective only states what not to do. If a behavioral objective states, "Do not speak when the teacher is speaking," any behavior other than speaking is established as acceptable when the teacher is speaking. When trying to modify behavior, this becomes very challenging if the desired behavior is not explicitly stated.

What to Do

- Consider desirable behaviors, and define them clearly.
- State the desirable behaviors clearly and in a positive way.
- Ensure that students are clear on the expectations through teaching and modeling.

Behavioral Outcomes—Positive and Negative

In the academic realm, there is a general structure of grading and promotion that is part of the educational system. Generally speaking, grades and promotion are tied to student performance of desired learning objectives. If a student meets the expectations, he or she achieves favorable grades and a promotion. If a student does not meet the expectations, he or she does not earn favorable grades and is not promoted. In the behavioral realm, the system is much less consistent and there is no established global protocol. Rewards and negative consequences for behaviors vary widely. Therefore, it is important that students are also clear about the behavior system in terms of meeting and not meeting the expectations.

Providing rewards and negative consequences is more effective if done consistently so that students are clear about expectations. The rewards and negative consequences should be logical and appropriate. Logical means that a negative consequence should be directly related to the undesired action. The reward should also be related to achievement of the desired behavioral objective. For example, a student has demonstrated understanding of a behavioral expectation related to when it is appropriate to talk. This student may be rewarded with an extra opportunity to talk to friends. A student who has not demonstrated the ability to meet that objective may be required to remain silent when others are allowed to talk. This example is certainly more simplistic than the reality of schools, but it illustrates a way of thinking about the logical element of rewards and consequences.

Rewards and consequences are dependent on the resources available as well as the students and their environment. In some ways, they are personal to a culture and within a community. What may be a reward for one population may be a negative consequence for another. This is also true for individual students as well. It is important to take into consideration the population of students to be addressed with the behavior plan. Values, resources, and culture all impact these decisions.

QUALITY INSTRUCTION

After establishing a quality core curriculum and behavior plan, the stage is set for instruction and the learning process. Planning and preparation are essential in the delivery of the core curriculum. Together, the instructional delivery and learning opportunities are considered a focused component of the processes of both RTI and DI. The quality core curriculum must be delivered through research-based strategies and practices to provide the best opportunities for students to achieve. This does not mean that all instruction must stem from published programs that have supporting research documentation. While these programs may be beneficial to students, their learning should not be limited only to published products. Instructional delivery should include instructional strategies that teachers know to be effective. These include opportunities for students to explore and discuss ideas, opportunities for movement and interaction, reinforcements of learning through multiple modalities, and added opportunities for practice to reinforce accurate learning.

Students respond differently to different learning opportunities. Some catch on quickly, while others take longer. Some need additional supports in order to experience success. At Tier 1, the recognition and response to these differences are processes of DI. An RTI framework acknowledges that within a classroom there are differences that need to be addressed through high-quality instruction, which includes differentiation. These differences and needs are identified through the collection of data. Prior to instruction, screening instruments and pre-assessments reflect some of the differences between students within a class, grade level, or school. The practice and methods implemented in response to those results include adapting both the curriculum and instruction to meet the needs of students. This is the essence of DI, and at Tier 1 it is found in the classroom frequently.

SCENARIO

Mrs. Barnes is a third-grade teacher. She is ready to begin a new school year. At the opening teachers' meeting, she is presented with assessment results from the past spring's standardized assessment. The scores include information regarding reading and mathematics skills. Along with the other third-grade teachers, Mrs. Barnes begins to analyze the data, with a focus on identifying students who performed significantly higher or lower than others. She and her grade-level team identify a group of several students who struggle with reading. They also identify a second group of students who struggle with mathematics.

The information provided tells Mrs. Barnes and the other teachers on her team that there seem to be more lower-performing math students in her class, while the teacher next door has all the students who perform exceedingly high in mathematics. They also notice that the student performances in reading cover the full spectrum in all classrooms. This leads Mrs. Barnes and the teachers to discuss potential collaboration. Mrs. Barnes and Mrs. Menard, the teacher next door, discuss doing some coteaching and flexible grouping in math so that the students in their classes can receive targeted instruction based on performance levels. The whole third-grade team considers planning a reading block at the same time so that they can allow students to switch classes for reading based on the targeted areas of strength and need in reading.

The third-grade teachers also consider the students they believe may be struggling readers. They are concerned about the new science textbook that seems to be written at a difficult reading level. Together, they determine strategies, accommodations, and resources that they could use in their classrooms to provide supports in science. They also discuss strategies that may be provided if they have learners who are high-achieving or who have already reached mastery of the content.

All of these discussions are done to prepare for the coming school year. They will set the stage for more conversations throughout the year. At this point, the teachers are working under the notion that they will be responsible for the successful learning for all third graders. They are not looking at additional personnel to assist with this and are instead considering the benefits of collaboration and necessity for differentiation of instruction. Once the students are in classes, the teachers will administer pre-assessments of their own to determine students' skills, strengths, and needs. The initial data from the previous year provide simply a baseline with which to predict possible areas of supports and challenge needed. The data are also a possible precursor signaling which students may raise concerns.

Once the students arrive in third grade, those who performed much higher or lower than others on the standardized test will be monitored starting on the first day of school. The third-grade teachers will determine whether the assessment results reflect accurate, current student performance. During the first week of school, Mrs. Barnes and her peers will identify how these specific students score on the initial assessments. While all the students will be assessed and their performances recorded, these students, who already have been tagged as students of concern, will be specifically noted.

DIFFERENTIATION FOR STRUGGLING LEARNERS WITHIN TIER 1

In the scenario above, Mrs. Barnes and her team are planning for the differentiation of instruction. They recognize that students will be at different knowledge and ability levels. For each to be successful, the teachers will need to provide accommodations and supports to some students. The basis for the decisions related to this will be the assessment information given before the beginning of the year, the pre-assessments, and the ongoing formative assessments during instruction.

RTI and DI are both focused on meeting students' needs in the classroom. Therefore, even within Tier 1, it is expected that accommodations and other supports will be implemented to provide the best opportunities for student success. These accommodations and supports are aligned to specific student needs and are not just random instructional strategies to help students gain mastery of content. They are a response to student performance. At this point, the "response" refers to the response *to* the student as much as it does to the response *of* the student.

In order to appropriately respond to students by providing additional supports, some processing must be done to ensure that the supports are logical and necessary. These supports should only be provided when needed and should not result in any unfair advantage. Following are some accommodations or supports that align to common needs in student performances:

If a student has a short attention span . . .

- Move around to make use of proximity.
- Provide individualized "To Do" and "Done" baskets so the student has a definite completion point.
- Consider placing the "Done" basket in a place requiring the student to walk over to it in order to give a movement break.
- Break the work into smaller parts on different pages or in different areas in the room.
- Use a picture cuing system to indicate start and stop.
- Provide an hourglass or visual timer so the "finish line" can be seen.
- Highlight important ideas using a verbal cue such as "This is a very important statement."
- Provide seating in a spot with fewer distractions or less traffic.
- Provide opportunities for multiple responses, such as response cards or electronic response systems.

If a student lacks conceptual skills, does not have background knowledge, or has a language barrier . . .

- Provide picture supports.
- Locate video or a website to provide virtual experience.

- Allow the student to preconference with a peer who is familiar with the concept or related concepts.
- Use different materials at a lower level.
- Provide an audio or video recording to review the lesson a second time.
- Adjust the vocabulary.
- Partner the student with someone who can translate and restate.

If a student struggles to remember a fact or complete a skill . . .

- Provide visual cues on the walls in an organized, resourceful system so that the student can know where to look for a cue and use the cues as a resource.
- Provide manipulatives.
- Provide additional practice using software or other technology.
- Use mnemonic devices.
- Provide graphic representations.
- Associate the unknown with something very familiar.
- Allow the student to take home an independent activity on the fact or skill for practice.
- Use explicit think-aloud strategies to provide metacognitive guidance when reviewing.
- Enlist peer supports for cuing or quizzing.
- Provide self-correcting activities for independent practice.
- Involve parents in supporting more practice opportunities.

If a student struggles with the organization of classroom routine . . .

- Provide an individual picture schedule.
- Use color-coded folders, binders, and systems that relate to the appropriate routine.
- Have the student repeat directions to a peer.
- Provide cues in the classroom related to the appropriate activity and time.
- Provide the student with a bin in which to place unneeded materials away from work area.
- Use tabs, and place them in books before instruction.
- Provide a consistent place to look for any directions, page numbers, and so on.

While these do not cover all the situations within a classroom, they are some of the common areas in which students need additional supports in order to be successful. All of the strategies listed above could be potential responses to what a student needs as reflected by his or her performance. Some of these strategies have been described simply as good teaching techniques. When they become intentional and systematic, aligned to a particular student need, the strategies go beyond good teaching and become responsive teaching.

DIFFERENTIATION FOR HIGH-ABILITY AND GIFTED LEARNERS WITHIN TIER 1

Thus far, the focus has been on students who struggle to achieve success with a particular learning objective. There are, however, students who face a challenge of a different kind. These are students who are high-ability and/or gifted and have mastered the material before instruction is ever provided. They too need additional supports and services to achieve their highest potential. In the age of "no child left behind," this is the group most likely to still be left, maybe not behind, but wherever they happen to be.

Results from screening data may indicate that a student is performing quite high in relation to expectations and benchmarks. This does not indicate a lack of need, but rather reflects a different type of need—a need for further data to be collected in order to see how high the student is already performing. In many cases, the initial information provided to teachers reflects mastery, but the instruments have ceilings and do not reflect how far above mastery the student really is. Therefore, off-grade-level assessments or assessments that go beyond the benchmark may be needed. Once it is known where the student peaks, the need can be identified. This need will be in terms of challenges rather than supports. These challenges may be in the form of additional depth or complexity, more rigorous investigations and exploration, or advanced content.

Within Tier 1, it is expected that differentiation will occur to support these students as well. Adjustments and expectations at Tier 1 should be provided to increase the levels of depth or complexity, rigor, or pace of learning. This can be done through accommodations. Within Tier 1, the following accommodations can be provided to students who are in need of additional challenges:

- Rather than simply recognizing patterns that exist in a variety of settings, the student identifies those patterns and uses them to predict future trends, outcomes, or events. The student may also create his or her own patterns, with emphasis placed on the complexity of the patterns.
- Rather than studying what the professional does in a discipline, the student actually does the work of that professional or with a professional. This may be done through the use of technology and webcams or actual communication directly between a professional and a student.
- Rather than looking for answers and facts for a topic, the student identifies new personal questions and questions that remain unanswered in a field of study.

- Rather than examining an event, person, or place, the student examines the relationship of that element to other elements over time. These may be established by the student, or they may be predetermined elements in which connections are made.
- Rather than establishing a viewpoint for a topic, the student takes an opposing or unusual point of view or perspective to examine the topic.
- Rather than completing an assignment as stated, an element is changed to challenge the student to consider "what if. . . ." For instance, if the class is learning about the life cycle of a frog, a student who already knows this can consider, what if the frog continued to have a tail throughout its development.

DIFFERENTIATION THROUGH GROUPING WITHIN TIER 1

Grouping can be an effective management strategy to meet the different needs of learners in the classroom. Groups can range in size from pairs to small groups of up to six or eight students. Research tells us that smaller groups are more effective than larger groups. Students working in pairs display more on-task behaviors and cause fewer conflicts (Gregory & Kuzmich, 2004). By identifying specific supports needed, those with common supports can be grouped to efficiently receive those supports. One of the differences between RTI and DI is grouping practices. Grouping for differentiated learning experiences allows for a variety of different types of groups. The reasons may be grouping for interest, learning styles, pace, background experiences, or preferences. Grouping for RTI is very specific and serves the purpose of providing small groups of students with the targeted supports and services needed for achievement. Within Tier 1, grouping may be done for any number of reasons; as part of a DI experience, it may be specifically to support learning needs.

In Tier 1, the most important aspect is not the delineation of the practice as being either part of RTI or DI. The grouping practices are one and the same. The important aspect of grouping in Tier 1 is the rationale for the grouping. Often grouping is used in combination with learning centers or as part of guided reading instruction. Using centers, small groups of students complete different activities without direct instruction while one group is working with the teacher to receive instruction or support. If these groups are formed through random selection, alphabetically by name, or by other means, it is a practice of neither RTI nor DI. It is a classroom management strategy. However, when these groups are formed based on a specific common attribute, it is considered DI.

When implementing grouping strategies, teachers must group students, even at Tier 1, because of an attribute they have in common. They may work at the same pace, have the same learning preference, or perform at the same achievement level. Any of these are appropriate. Research on cluster grouping, or grouping students by likenesses with a limited number of different attributes, has shown that this strategy fosters strong academic growth (Gentry, 1999). In Tier 1, all of the groups may be working with or without direct instructional support. If the grouping is done to provide learning supports, students are grouped by like performance levels and the teacher provides direct instruction to a small group. This instruction can be different for each of the groups and is directly targeted to the specific instructional needs of the students in each group. This is most commonly seen in guided reading groups. When establishing groups, there are several elements to consider:

- What is the desired learning outcome?
- Why is grouping being considered as a strategy? Classroom management? Targeted small-group instruction?
- What attribute(s) is being used to determine groupings?
- Are there social considerations or work habits to consider?
- How will materials be managed?
- Do students have clear expectations regarding roles and responsibilities when working in groups?

Need for Collaboration

Grouping strategies are used to meet the specific needs of learners in small-group settings. In order to provide that level of support, collaboration is critical. In any given classroom, there are many different student needs. If grouping is to be used to target those needs through direct small-group instruction, there may in fact be several small groups of students, each with different needs. With only one teacher in the classroom, it may be quite difficult to manage the groups and provide all the services needed. Most often, the teacher next door also struggles with the same issue. Therefore, there is a greater need for the two teachers to work together to help support each other's efforts.

Consider this example: Dr. Robertson is teaching mathematics to her fifth graders and is specifically focusing on adding fractions. When she considers her students and their levels of performance, she finds that some are struggling with the concept of fractions, a few are struggling with the concept of denominators, a few are struggling with the calculations required to convert the fractions into like denominators, and some are quite proficient at the standard. There is also one student who has missed the past four days of instruction and is in need of instruction from the beginning. If Dr. Robertson were to create small groups for instructional supports, she would need to have at least five different groups. She does not feel like she has the time to be able to work with five different groups. She also does not believe her students will be able to maintain focus on their group tasks while she focuses on three or four students at time. Her solution is to collaborate with Mr. McNaughton next door. He is also teaching math at the same time. Together, they have several students who struggle with the concept of fractions and several who struggle with creating like denominators for the purpose of adding. They each have a few students who have mastered the skill as well as many who have nearly mastered it.

Dr. Robertson and Mr. McNaughton arrange to combine all the students of the two classes for math on a given day each week. This particular week, Dr. Robertson creates a group of students from her class who need support with the concept of fractions. Mr. McNaughton sends over his students who need support with the same concept. Dr. Robertson provides targeted instruction to those students while Mr. McNaughton has responsibility for the rest of the students. He has the students working on high-motivation activities to reinforce math concepts that they can complete independently but with which they need additional practice. He also provides some advanced challenge for a small group of students who have mastered much of the curriculum already. During this time, they are able to work on mathematical concepts at a higher grade level.

On some days, Dr. Robertson is able to meet with two different groups through this model. There are other times when Mr. McNaughton takes the small groups for targeted instruction while Dr. Robertson takes the rest of the students. By working together and setting up this system, both Dr. Robertson and Mr. McNaughton are able to better support all of their students' learning and meet their needs.

SUMMARY

Tier 1 showcases the overlap of both RTI and DI. Both are focused on delivering high-quality instruction based on well-defined standards of a solid core curriculum. Both use student performance data as the pivotal factor in making instructional decisions. These decisions relate to issues such as presentation, student production, and levels of supports provided to individual students. These supports may include accommodations to meet the needs of struggling learners as well as those who need additional challenge. Grouping strategies assist in the management of meeting the variety of student needs in the classroom, and collaboration is an effective tool in the implementation of grouping.

QUESTIONS TO CONSIDER

- Where do your standards come from? Who wrote them? What research were they based on?
- Do your standards align to the national standards within a discipline?
- Are the standards currently in use measurable and clearly defined in terms of mastery?
- Are there specific indicators to know when mastery is met? Can you define the benchmarks along the way to mastery that should indicate progress in the learning process?
- Once standards are determined as facts or skills, what efforts are made and resources in place to create independent leveled practice in the form of centers, technology-based opportunities, and contract work for students?
- Are behavioral expectations stated positively? Are they clearly defined? Are students clear about the behavioral expectations?
- Are the behavioral expectations the same in different settings within the school? Are they enforced consistently and to the same degree?
- What summative assessment results do you have access to before planning instructional delivery?
- What assessments do you have students complete as pre-assessments?
- What accommodations are most often considered for struggling learners? Are there accommodations that you have not considered that may be helpful?
- How do you meet the needs of learners who come into the class already having mastery of the standards? What accommodations do you most frequently provide for these students?
- What structures do you use to determine small groups? How do you manage small groups in your classroom? Have you considered collaborating with another teacher?
- What benefits are there for teachers who collaborate with each other? What benefits are there for the students?

5

Tier 1—Assessment

The essence of data is 50% about providing answers and 50% about prompting new questions. If we only look at data to answer questions, we have missed half of its function.

WHAT TYPES OF ASSESSMENT RESULTS DO WE EXAMINE?

In Tier 1, assessment data are examined in many ways. The data paint the picture, tell the story, and create the plans for the future. They also prompt new questions and ideas. The examination of data in Tier 1 is no less detailed than in other tiers. It is the perspective that is different. At Tier 1, data are viewed through a wider lens. At this stage, questions and investigations involve the whole school, the whole grade level, and the whole class. This wide-angle lens helps to identify areas of need. Looking at data in Tier 1 also focuses on individual students and their strengths and needs. Tier 1 has several different perspectives when it comes to examining data. Each has a different purpose, and together they all help to provide information for use in decision making. Table 5.1 shows the lenses used in Tier 1 to examine data.

Table 5.1   Examining Data in Tier 1

Type of Data Examination	Data Indicators
Whole-school data Standardized data that help compare student performance in one school to student performance in other schools	• Show trends across the school in specific content areas • Show content areas that need the most focus • Guide goal setting used in the school improvement plan for yearlong goals
Grade-level data Standardized data that help compare students across a grade level to other students in the grade within the school and outside the school	• Show trends within a grade level at a particular school • Show specific strands within content areas that need the most focus • Show the individual students at each grade level who have the greatest need for supports and services • Guide teams of content area teachers in creating areas of focus for long-term goals
Classroom data Standardized data and other valid assessments that show the performance of students in the same class	• Show the performance range and trends of students in a classroom • Guide instructional focus for the class • Guide the differentiated instructional decision making that occurs regularly in the classroom
Individual student data Standardized and valid assessments that show the performance of a particular student in any number of areas	• Show the performance of a student in different content areas, settings, or learning opportunities • Guide instructional decisions regarding materials, teaching strategies, and modes of communication within the process of learning and the product • Guide decisions regarding the amount of support and challenge to be provided

SCENARIO

It is the first week of school, and Mrs. Schall has learned the names of her new third-grade students, but at this point she is working to learn more about them. She has observed her students this first week and made some notes about some of them. She has discovered that some students do not work well together, some take over the project when assigned to do group work, and others sit back and do nothing. Mrs. Schall has also recognized students who are self-motivated learners, deep thinkers, and people who work well in different cooperative settings. During this first week she administered some pre-assessments to determine the knowledge that the students have brought to the classroom along with some initial benchmark assessments based on what the standards are for the year to come.

Mrs. Schall brings this information with her when she goes to her team meeting so that the teachers can discuss the students and study the data. This will assist them in their decision making and planning for any collaborative groups they may want to create. Mrs. Schall is on a team with three other third-grade teachers and a speech language pathologist. The school reading coach also participates with the team as much as possible.

At this first team meeting, the teachers focus on reading and language arts. Each of the teachers comes with their students' standardized test scores. They map out these scores to determine the overall performance by grade level. It is clear from doing this activity that the grade as a whole is strong in the area of decoding but weak in the area of reading for meaning and comprehension. The guidance counselor who has joined them confirms that these results are consistent across the school. She informs this team that there will be a school literacy committee meeting to discuss schoolwide efforts to increase comprehension skills. The third-grade team will have representation on that committee. As a team, the teachers determine that their first step will be to create an action plan that focuses on comprehension for students at their grade level. They examine the data by grade level more specifically. They see that while comprehension is an area of concern and decoding is strong in general, there are some subpopulations in which this is not the case. The data show that some students did poorly in both areas, and it seems that students with disabilities did better as a group with comprehension than decoding. While it seemed at first glance that all third graders needed to focus on comprehension, further examination shows other critical areas in as much need for certain groups of students.

Now, along with the other professionals on her team, Mrs. Schall looks at her classroom data to begin making decisions regarding her differentiation of instruction. The students in her class who did poorly on their standardized testing will likely need additional supports in the classroom. Mrs. Schall knows that she will be responsible for providing those supports. She does not assume that all of these students will be in need of supports through additional interventions, and she knows her abilities to differentiate instruction will be the first step. The other third-grade teachers also know that they will need to differentiate their instruction as well. At this point, they have not determined that any student is in need of additional interventions beyond what is done in the classroom. The teachers may find that there are students who do need more, as determined through data to be looked at later. For now, the teachers simply begin to consider their part in supporting the students.

(Continued)

(Continued)

Mrs. Schall begins by looking at the results of the initial reading screening she administered since it has the most direct connection to her upcoming instructional focus.

The results of the pre-assessment have given Mrs. Schall a foundation with which to begin to sort her students in terms of ability and readiness to learn the new standards. She uses the results to create three groups of students. She has one list of students who seem to be proficient in many or all of the prerequisite skills she had hoped they would have. She has a second list of students who seem to be lacking in some important skill areas and have relative strength in other areas. She has a third list of students who performed very poorly and reflect a lack of most of the skill areas assessed.

Mrs. Schall then refers to the standardized test scores from the previous year to see if those results align with her pre-assessment results. She expects the students in List 1 to be in the top quartile on the test results, those in List 2 to be somewhere in the top half, and those in List 3 to be below the 50th percentile. For any of her students who do not align with these expectations, Mrs. Schall makes a note to indicate whether they performed higher or lower on the standardized testing than she would have expected. Now she is ready to examine her data in more depth. This information will help her make decisions regarding her plans for differentiated instruction as well as possible additional supports that may be needed for students to be challenged at appropriate levels and to experience success in her classroom.

Mrs. Schall begins with List 1. She goes back to look at actual items on the pre-assessment and the student responses. She looks specifically for indicators of levels of mastery. These are her questions for each pre-assessment:

- Are there indicators that reflect performance that is already at mastery of content not yet covered?
- Are there any areas in which there appear to be deficiencies?
- Are there indicators of specific strengths in any areas?

Mrs. Schall asks these questions because she knows there are students in this group who will need to have additional challenges and enrichment opportunities for more depth and complexity in their learning. She also knows that a student with a high score may need additional instruction and may still have areas of need that are compensated for by areas of strength. Mrs. Schall makes an indicator for any students on this list who seem to have already mastered the specific content that will be covered in upcoming lessons, creating a need for additional challenges and learning opportunities. Those students are put into a sublist labeled Potential Needs for Additional Challenge, or AC for short. For students who demonstrate some areas that are specific strengths or areas of need in this group, she notes these on her list and they remain on the original List 1.

Mrs. Schall then moves on to the second group of students, List 2. These are students who performed satisfactorily in some areas and poorly in other areas, indicating a need for additional supports. She looks at the actual items carefully to identify any patterns here, and she asks the following questions:

- Are there areas that seem to be consistently strong while others tend to be weak for many students?
- Are there areas in which there are errors in skills that can be easily reviewed?
- Are there areas involving significant conceptual understandings that are lacking?

Mrs. Schall then creates a sublist of skills and objectives assessed that involve any areas on the pre-assessment that reflect the relative strengths for the group and areas that seemed consistently weak. She also examines each individual's performance and indicates on her list the areas of strength and need for each of the students on List 2.

Finally, Mrs. Schall moves to List 3. These are students whose performance on her pre-assessment reflect a lack of most of the prerequisite skills needed to be successful in her class. She predicts that these students will be in need of substantial additional supports in order to be successful. Mrs. Schall looks at the items of each pre-assessment and asks the following questions:

- Was there an attempt to respond to each item, or do responses reflect effort on the part of the student?
- Do any answers reflect important misunderstandings of a significant concept that impacts multiple items on the assessment?
- Do any responses raise concerns about the student's ability that far exceed concerns about other students?

Mrs. Schall answers these questions to identify both learning and curricular issues that may become significant. She first indicates for each student any areas in which there are misunderstandings of specific concepts that seem to impact multiple areas. For instance, one student who was unable to identify a graphic of a water cycle as being such was also unable to complete comprehension questions that asked about changes to the water cycle process. A conceptual misunderstanding or inability such as this can have a major impact on an assessment score.

Mrs. Schall then creates sublists for these students as well. She first creates a sublist of any student who did not seem to try to attempt the items on the pre-assessment. These students will need further investigation to predict whether the lack of responses is due to lack of ability or lack of motivation. Mrs. Schall creates a second sublist for any student about whom she has immediate and glaring concerns. She will need to gather more information about these students in order to learn what supports may have been provided in the past or what factors contribute to the students' low performance.

It is significant to note here that Mrs. Schall did not immediately look at school records to identify which students had been identified as gifted and which had been identified as having a disability. The information she was interested in was the performance of the students in her classroom in relation to her curriculum. This does not mean that Mrs. Schall will not need to know that information. It will be important for her ultimately to review that information as well so that she will be able to provide supports and services that have been determined as necessary for student success. She will use that information in her instructional delivery to meet those students' needs and maintain compliance with state and federal rules and regulations regarding services for these students. However, at this point those data do not provide her with the depth of information she is seeking. At this point, in order to move forward with planning, Mrs. Schall needs information about the students in relation to a specific area rather than generalized learning characteristics.

SELECTING OR DEVELOPING SCREENING INSTRUMENTS

At the beginning of any school year, there is information that may be accessible and may help provide information about the overall strengths and needs of students. In most cases, this is "big picture" information. The data are often in the form of standardized assessments and previous report card grades. In some instances, teachers may also have access to work samples using student portfolios. However, in most cases teachers receive only a snapshot or two of each student.

Therefore, after establishing a clear understanding of the desired learning outcomes, the next step is to determine the knowledge, abilities, conceptions, and misconceptions that students have in relation to those desired learning outcomes. This information is best obtained through the use of a screening instrument that is matched to the outcomes. The screening instrument is administered to students with the intent of gaining insight into the their thinking, knowledge, strengths, and needs related to upcoming instruction. It is not intended to be graded. In some cases, publishers have screening assessments available and aligned to the textbook. These may be a great tool for identifying both the skills and concepts students have in relation to the upcoming learning. Because they are *upcoming* learning experiences, there is not an expectation that students will reflect mastery on the screening instruments. The purpose of the tool is insight, not evaluation.

There are several important factors to consider when selecting a screening assessment. The consideration of each of these factors is critical in the effectiveness of the practice. Using a broad screening instrument that has not been carefully examined can wind up providing no more information than a set of typical standardized test results. A screening is administered for the purpose of providing content- and standard-specific information related to the curriculum. Not considering these factors is like using a globe instead of a map to plot a route for a trip. A traveler will have a relative idea of where he or she is going but no real definitive plan for how to get there.

When choosing a screening instrument, the first thing to consider is the alignment of the instrument to the objectives. One commonly used tool is the screening instrument provided by publishers. It is important to look critically at these published assessments, though. Unless the text is completely aligned to the learning objectives of the curriculum, there may be objectives that are assessed and not addressed in the curriculum and other objectives in the curriculum that are not present on the assessment. Also, there are several versions of a textbook produced by the same company for any particular grade level, and publishers have various requirements for different states and regions. Therefore there is variation between textbooks even from the same publisher. If there is a single screening instrument developed for all versions of the text, there may be objectives missing or others that are assessed even though they may not be part of the curriculum. Therefore, it is important to look carefully at the assessment tool to ensure that your desired learning objectives are actually the ones addressed within the screening instrument.

A second thing to consider when using a published screening instrument is whether it will provide you with the information you want to know. Even if you are going to study the life cycle of a frog, you need to first identify the skills and concepts you will be addressing through instruction and then match those to the screening instrument. In some cases, your desired learning outcome will be one perspective of a content area, while the screening is designed to provide you with very different information. For instance, Mrs. Schall wants to know the students' abilities related to verbs, so she wants to know if they can both use them and identify them. Many assessments will do one or the other but not both. Your screening instrument must be matched to the information you desire and need to drive your instruction.

A third factor to consider with the use of a published screening instrument is the validity of the instrument itself. This does not mean that it needs to be norm-referenced or standardized in any way. It means that the assessment must have prompts that are reliable in providing the information you want to obtain. There should be no trick questions. There should also be few, if any, matching of banks so that answers to some questions depend on others. Doing so allows for guessing rather than accurate communication of knowledge. For the same reason, closed-ended questions should be limited. The best screening instruments are those that are open-ended. Although these take longer to evaluate and process, they certainly provide the most valuable information.

Finally, another important criterion is that the screening must cover the facts, skills, and concepts related to an idea. Procedural or informational knowledge is different from conceptual knowledge. Both are necessary for mastery in any content area. Both can be reflected in isolation and appear to convey mastery. Without evidence of both conceptual understanding and procedural or informational understanding, questions will remain as to a student's level of mastery.

The best screening instrument is one that is matched to the desired learning objectives; that communicates clearly what each student knows, believes, and is able to do; and that provides information about the thinking of each student. It should be open-ended and easy for a teacher to process, and it should provide valuable information about desired learning outcomes.

So how is this achieved if the screening instrument created by the publisher is not appropriate or sufficient? Here are some suggestions for developing questions or prompts for a screening instrument:

1. Change the objective into a question. For instance, the desired learning objective is "Students will see the relationship between addition and subtraction." That can easily be changed to "What is the relationship between addition and subtraction?"

2. Allow for a variety of forms of communication. For example, if the objective is recognition of the relationship between addition and subtraction, allow students to communicate that relationship in words, drawings, or numeric symbols. In grammar, allow students to describe it, provide examples, or identify the grammar within an existing sentence.

3. Provide questions that address the facts, skills, and conceptual understandings of an objective. If the objective is related to the mastery of verbs, the prompt should allow students to define a verb, use a verb, identify a verb, and discuss the role that verbs play in communication. This may be presented through a quadrant graphic such as the example below, which addresses the learning objective demonstrating the relationship between addition and subtraction.

Complete these problems: $25 - 12 =$ $14 + 9 =$	What is addition?	What does subtract mean?
Show what these look like in pictorial form: $12 - 8 = 4$ and $4 + 8 = 12$	How are addition and subtraction opposites?	

4. Keep items distinct and separate so that instruction can be targeted specifically to the areas of need or misunderstandings. In the example above, each task is distinct yet communicates vital information related to the learning objective. Each box addresses a skill or a specific concept. This assessment pinpoints a student's understanding of the concepts of addition, subtraction, and the relationship between addition and subtraction. It also assesses the skills of simply adding and subtracting. By creating discrete questioning, teachers can help students communicate knowledge, understandings, and misunderstandings in a way that makes it easy to identify needs for instruction.

5. Include prerequisite understandings in the screening. In the example above, the skills of adding and subtracting are prerequisites to understanding the relationship of the two. By assessing the prerequisite knowledge of adding and subtracting, the tool provides information regarding a starting point for needed instruction.

6. Do not include instruction within the screening instrument. The screening tool is not a place for teaching or reteaching. There should be no long explanations or directions. The screening instrument is to gain awareness of what a student can recall and process without instruction or guidance. Providing opportunities to build background knowledge is part of the instructional process, not part of the screening assessment process.

Taking further the analogy of a screening instrument being likened to a map, the screening instrument is like a map of a state. It allows a teacher to establish an estimated sense of time and distance. However, it will not provide specifics related to the trip itself. The screening instrument is the tool to begin to plan the trip. It will not be the only tool used on the trip, nor will it provide the most detail. What it does provide is a very practical starting point once the destination has been determined.

PROCESSING THE RESULTS OF SCREENING INSTRUMENTS

After developing (or choosing) the screening instrument aligned to the learning objectives, the teacher administers the assessment to the students. The next step is to make sense of the information collected through the assessment. This takes time, and there are several stages to the process. The screening instrument should not be scored and put into a file with a numeric total entered into a grade book. Instead, the information should be dissected and processed in order to become practical in directing the instructional pathways.

The items on the screening assessment should be evaluated item by item. Each should be recorded based on performance. For instance, in the example above pertaining to addition and subtraction, the chart in Table 5.2 would be completed.

Although this takes time and a great deal of recording, it becomes useful when developing the instructional plans. It also reflects specific areas in which instruction is needed by all students and where there is great disparity in the performance levels.

After recording the results of the screening assessment, the next step is to make an overall comparison between the score on the screening assessment and the other data that are accessible for individual students. The purpose is to identify any significant discrepancies between the two results. If there are discrepancies, more information will need to be obtained for an accurate picture. However, if a student scores well on a screening instrument and also scores well on the standardized test, there

Table 5.2   Evaluation Chart for Assessment on Addition and Subtraction

	Student A	Student B	Student C	Student D	Student E	Student F
Calculating addition						
Calculating subtraction						
Definition of addition						
Definition of subtraction						
Concept of addition (from the pictorial element)						
Concept of subtraction (from the pictorial element)						
Concept of relationship of addition and subtraction as opposites						

is a level of certainty that the information is valid. Likewise, if a student scores well on the screening but very poorly on the standardized test, there are questions to be answered in relation to the difference in performance. In the earlier scenario, Mrs. Schall completed this step by comparing her screening results to the standardized test scores from the year before.

USING THE SCREENING DATA TO INFORM INSTRUCTION

After the data have been processed and disaggregated, instructional planning can take place. The information from the screening provides insight into a starting point for instruction as well as areas in which the whole class needs supports and instructional guidance. It also provides a framework for grouping students in guided instructional groups. The information allows for instruction to act as a platform based on what a student already knows and as a criterion for moving into new knowledge. This benefits all students, including those who are in the higher levels of performance. Based on information about students' level of understanding or mastery of certain concepts, instruction can be designed to accelerate or enrich experiences for these students.

Here in the instructional planning phase, differentiation is anticipated as needed and a teacher can prepare for the expected needs. The screening information allows a teacher to target needed prerequisite skills and facts for a new concept. In most cases, the screening results will indicate that students are performing at different levels. Using the earlier example, there may be six students who show a conceptual understanding of the relationship between addition and subtraction and eighteen who reflect the need for more instruction simply on the skills of addition and subtraction. There may also be five students who need additional support on the definition of what addition really means. Therefore, before instruction on the relationship of addition and subtraction, a small group should be formed with those five students so that the teacher can review or reteach what addition is. Without that foundation, the planned lesson will be completely lost on them. This small-group instruction reviewing what addition really means can be done at the beginning of the period while other students are working independently on adding and subtracting skills as practice for the upcoming related lesson.

The second use of screening data to approach instruction is application of the results to determine where to begin developing a conceptual understanding. While the curriculum guide may tell a teacher that he or she needs to be teaching about the relationship between addition and subtraction, the screening information may make it clear that prerequisite skills must be addressed before beginning the originally intended instruction. DI requires teachers to identify where the student is in relation to the standard and then meet the student at that level and move the student forward toward the desired outcome.

PROGRESS MONITORING AND FORMATIVE ASSESSMENT DURING INSTRUCTION

Progress monitoring and formative assessment are critical elements of Tier 1 instruction in a Response to Instruction/Intervention (RTI) process. Together, they are a cornerstone of differentiated instruction (DI). The data from assessments and instructional decisions create the appropriate learning experiences for students. These two types of assessments are critical in the classroom and are an important part of the Tier 1 assessments involved in RTI.

It is a common misconception that progress monitoring and formative assessment are one and the same. In an RTI model, they are different and serve very different purposes. Progress monitoring is frequent data collection for the purpose of looking for movement or growth in learning. Progress monitoring assessments are implemented to track student progress. These indicators tell an educator if a student is making appropriate growth and at what rate. Formative assessment also includes the practice of frequent data collection, but the purpose is to use data to make instructional decisions. The indicators of formative assessment can show when instruction needs to be slowed, accelerated, retaught, or used to move forward. Both types of assessment provide an objective base for decision making.

Progress Monitoring

Progress monitoring serves several purposes in an RTI framework as well as within the process of differentiating instruction. It provides a measure of effectiveness of instruction and guides instructional decision making. It establishes an expectation of performance over time and determines the rate of improvement. Without progress monitoring, there is no way to determine if learning gains are going to be rapid enough to close a learning gap. There are some distinct characteristics of progress monitoring and the practices of collecting data for progress monitoring. Progress monitoring data should be all of the following:

- frequent
- consistent in format and intervals of collection
- quantifiable
- recorded as a series and compared with other data over time
- used to compare the rate of student learning to each student along with peers

Frequent

The data collection for progress monitoring should be frequent in order for the data to indicate changes in growth or rate. These indicators can be formal or informal. Electronic clickers are an easy way to collect frequent data on an individual basis. These response systems can track individual student responses and will display results for each student. Other simple measures include strategies such as exit cards. Each student responds to a prompt designed to be completed at the end of a class period. The card has the student's name, and it is turned in on the way out the door. In this way, data can be recorded to indicate, from day to day, how a student responds to a prompt.

Consistent

Progress monitoring data collection is not designed to trick students. The purpose is to measure student growth. Therefore, to be most valid in reflecting growth, the data should be collected in the same way each day. The format of the progress monitoring should be consistent. For instance, if Monday's progress monitoring prompt is to name five characteristics of a plant and Tuesday's is to name five characteristics of a mammal, the data do not reveal any growth in the understanding of a concept. Instead, if Monday's question stays the same, Tuesday's prompt may be to name three characteristics common to both a plant and an animal. This assumes that the characteristics of an animal have been provided, of course.

Because the purpose is to measure incremental changes, data collection must be done at regularly scheduled intervals. There is no standard amount of time between collected data, but the collection should be at the same intervals each time. For instance, data may be collected once a day for two weeks or it may be collected once every two days for twenty days. The important part is to collect the data consistently. Data should not be randomly collected so that there are indicators a few days in a row and then not for a few days, then one day of data and then none for another two days. The time period between each data collection should remain constant.

Quantifiable

In order for the data to be manageable and an indicator of progress, the data must be able to be recorded numerically. This may be in the form of points awarded for an answer, a specific numeric score, or even a proportion between the number of correct items and the total number of items. No matter what form is used, it needs to be consistent. The purpose is to measure, so a consistent measuring increment is needed in order to have data that communicate growth or change.

Recording and Making Comparisons Over Time

The point of progress monitoring data is to reveal changes over time. Therefore, the data must be recorded and tracked. The only way to see whether changes have occurred is if multiple indicators are present. These indicators should be recorded in a format that allows for trends to be seen. Progress monitoring data are most effective when recorded separately from other data.

Comparing Data

Progress monitoring reflects the progress made by a student over time. The data indicate the rate at which the change or growth is taking place. This rate is then compared to the rate at which other learning is occurring or has occurred for the student. For instance, data may be collected to see how frequently new math facts are acquired using a new software program that provides additional practice. Data may show that before the program was used, the student learned new math facts at a rate of two per week. Then data after using the program show that the same student is now acquiring math facts at four per week. These data encourage the teacher to continue to provide time for the student to use the software.

The rate of progress is also compared to the rate of growth of other students. For instance, the student above learned new facts at a rate of four per week, which contrasts with other students learning an average of five per week. The progress monitoring data show that the student learning only four per week is going to fall further behind at the current rate of progress.

Formative Assessment

Like progress monitoring, formative assessment data are collected frequently and regularly. However, there are some significant differences in the data collection. Formative assessment is primarily used by a teacher to guide instructional decision making. Therefore, in some cases formative assessments may be implemented and not recorded. Generally, formative assessment is embedded in the learning process. An example is the teacher's use of electronic response systems or personal whiteboards throughout the instructional process. The teacher does not record the data in a grade book but uses the data to see whether students understand the instruction. The assessment is very often informal in nature and can be as simple as listening to students' responses when they share with each other. Formative assessment does not necessarily predict performance outcomes. It is used to form instruction, rather than simply to inform. Finally, while progress monitoring is most often implemented after a lesson or instructional series, formative assessment is implemented during the instruction. The formative assessment becomes part of the instruction itself. Checking progress at intervals makes it more likely that the instruction is producing desired results (Gregory & Kuzmich, 2004).

When evaluating responses in formative assessment measures at any of the tiers, there are three possible categories of response. Students may provide correct responses, in which case it can be determined that the instruction was effective. Students may respond with a questionable response, which means there is uncertainty about their proficiency, ability, or need for additional instruction or support. Or students may provide an incorrect response or a lack of a positive response, in which case further analysis must be conducted to investigate the reason or cause of the poor response.

Error Analysis

One of the key processes extending from formative assessment is error analysis. When a student or group of students makes errors, these errors must be examined the same way a doctor examines a patient complaining of a pain. The doctor asks questions and explores the area in which a problem may be occurring. The teacher does the same type of exploration. The purpose is to target the source of the problem. Curing or solving the problem comes later. First, the question to ask is, "What is not right?" Next would be a question about the cause. Once the cause is targeted, changes can be made or supports put in place to rectify the situation.

SCENARIO

Mr. Russell is teaching a math class. The learning objective is "Students will be able to accurately subtract two digit numbers." After he provides instruction, the students complete three problems independently. Mr. Russell looks at the students' responses. Many of the students have correct answers, but a significant number of students have incorrect answers on all three. Most have the same incorrect answers. These students with errors have the following responses:

$$52 - 34 = 22 \qquad 61 - 48 = 27 \qquad 58 - 19 = 41$$

Mr. Russell looks at these incorrect responses for the purpose of identifying why the students arrived at the wrong answers. He recognizes that these students subtracted the larger digit from the smaller digit in the ones column with no regard to what number they were part of. When the students saw $2 - 4$ in the ones column, they just changed it to $4 - 2$ and derived an answer of 2. There was no regrouping the tens to create enough units in the ones place to subtract. By understanding what these students did wrong, he can reteach the skill targeting the common mistake.

USING THE TWO TYPES OF ASSESSMENT TO DIFFERENTIATE INSTRUCTION

While progress monitoring is used primarily to show students' growth and change over time, it lends itself mainly to grouping practices with DI. For the practicality of classroom management, along with striving for highest student achievement, progress monitoring can influence decisions related to grouping students. A group of students who the data indicate need additional support on a skill can be grouped together, while data may indicate that another group of students are ready to move to a more complex concept and thus can be grouped together. This is commonly referred to in reading as guided reading groups. The groups are created based on targeted skill needs.

Formative assessment also contributes to DI within grouping practices. As part of an instructional sequence, a teacher may group students who indicate through formative assessment that they can work independently while the teacher provides support to others who need additional supports. Besides grouping, formative assessment can assist in the process of DI by informing when the additional supports are needed and how much support may be required. Formative assessment provides insights into when accommodations should be implemented for particular students, when pacing should be slowed, or when teaching a concept in a different way may be needed. Formative assessment is truly embedded into the instructional process itself.

DATA USE AND MANAGEMENT IN TIER 1

It has been established that previously administered assessments and screening instruments provide initial information about students and contribute to the planning of instruction. Formative assessments are part of the instructional process and assist in appropriate implementation of instruction. Progress monitoring reflects the rate and growth of a student or students in response to the instruction. In some cases, diagnostic assessment information may also be available and contribute to the picture. Each of these assessments provides valuable information and opportunities for further questions. Useful data provides as many questions as it does answers. The questions that may be generated differ for each type of assessment (see Table 5.3).

For any data source that calls attention, there are also some general questions to ask:

- Do the data reflect a level of motivation that is exceedingly high or low?
- Do the data reflect a level of ability that is exceedingly high or low?
- Do the data reflect the need for more attention, supports, or services to be provided immediately?
- Are the data inconsistent? Is there a need for further investigation or more specific data?

Table 5.3 Questions to Consider for Various Assessment Data

Source of Data	Questions to Consider
Previous standardized test results	• Are there areas of strength for the student? • Are there areas of need? • Are the areas of strength and need consistent with other students? • Are the needs in areas that impact performance in other areas such as comprehension? • Are the data consistent? Do they show a trend with previous years' scores?
Previous report card grades	• Are grades consistent with indicators of performance reflected on standardized test results? • Are grades consistent across content areas? • Are any content area grades that are not consistent with other content areas consistent with other peers? (For example, a student shows all high grades except in science.) Is that the case for many other students as well?
Previous summative assessments	• Are the summative assessments from prior units of study consistent, or are there peaks and valleys? • If there are inconsistencies, what elements are in common with those units that lie outside the trend? • Do the summative assessments align with previous report card grades from other years of classroom production? • Are results of the summative assessments reflective of performance that is consistent with that of peers? For instance, did most students do very well or very poorly on a specific assessment?
Wide-scale or universal screening (e.g., grade-level assessment given to all students in a content area at the beginning of a school year, placement tests)	• Do the screening data reflect consistencies with the standardized test data? • Are there areas that seem to be consistent with peers? • Are there areas that are not consistent with peers? • Do the data reflect a student's performance compared to his or her peers?

(Continued)

Table 5.3 (Continued)

Pre-assessment	• Does the pre-assessment accurately assess the level of performance related to the desired learning outcome? • Do factors such as language or vocabulary influence the assessment? • Does the assessment rely on background experiences or prior knowledge? • Are the pre-assessment results consistent with other data sources? • Is the pre-assessment measure a valid assessment? • Was the pre-assessment administered with fidelity?
Formative assessments with error analysis	• Does the assessment have a match to the instruction? For instance, if students learn a skill with a specific procedure, does the assessment assess that same procedure? • Does the assessment reflect errors in common with multiple trials? • Does the assessment reflect errors in common with many peers? • Does the assessment reflect complete mastery and a lack of need for further instruction?
Progress monitoring	• Do the data compare the same indicators of a desired learning outcome over time? In other words, do the assessments compare apples to apples? • Do the data sets show clear trends of progress or lack of progress? • Is the rate of progress appropriate to maintain grade-level performance expectations?
Diagnostics	• Does the assessment target specific areas of concern? • Do the results answer questions about ability, motivators, triggers for negative behavior, or areas of strength? • Do the results seem consistent with other assessment measures? • Are the data specific enough to create a statement to be used to design a plan of action?

PUTTING THE DATA PIECES TOGETHER

Now that the types of assessment in Tier 1 have been established, how do these assessments work together in Tier 1 of RTI to establish the supports and services a student may need?

The screening assessments give a snapshot of a student's abilities or performance. This information is used as a platform. There are some students whose screening results raise questions or concerns; these students are flagged. This simply means there is a reason to ask questions. The questions may be addressed to the teachers from the previous year, administrators or guidance counselors, the family, or the student himself or herself. A flag also indicates that there is reason to monitor the student more closely than others. This flag prevents the student from falling through the cracks or being missed in the system. A student who is flagged may never, in fact, have any problems. The flag does not mean "problem" or "danger" or "warning." It simply means "keep watch."

In the beginning of the year and at designated times throughout the year, teachers should have opportunities to ask questions about each student who has been flagged. Each student should have assessment results, and these should be reviewed. A review may determine that the student had a difficult time with a specific assessment but demonstrates competency on all other assessments. These reviews may also indicate significant reasons for concern. Any student who has been flagged and who has been determined to be of concern should be marked as an individual to watch closely through data collection and by gathering more information. This does not mean the student needs additional supports and services through a more intensive tier, but rather needs to be watched closely.

These students of concern should have frequent progress monitoring indicators that are recorded and tracked by the classroom teacher as part of instructional practices. The progress monitoring data should be able to indicate whether the student is experiencing success in learning or needs additional supports. There are three elements of data to consider for any student about whom there are concerns:

- Is the student showing progress?
- Is the rate of progress allowing the student to keep up with instruction?
- Is the student's progress different than that of his or her peers?

If the answer to any of these questions is "no" or "questionable," the teacher must respond and provide DI through the use additional supports and accommodations. The teacher may also provide some additional supports in the form of reteaching or reinforcements to increase the level of prerequisite skills needed for success. Small-group instruction with students who have similar needs is also appropriate. (These strategies are all part of DI and best practices that were discussed in Chapter 4.) It is important to note that any change to instruction, program, or support should be based on the data. Any change should also provide instructional practices, programs, or methods of instruction that are based on evidence or research. No change should be arbitrary. The following are some questions to guide change:

Error Analysis

- Why is the error occurring? Does the student have the prerequisite skills? Background knowledge? Vocabulary? Motivation? Conceptual understanding?
- Where is the error occurring? Approaching the task? During the task? Communicating the results?

Decision Making

- What research- or evidence-based strategies, programs, or instruction aligns to the deficit?
- How and when will you know if the change is effective?

While providing these additional supports for struggling students, the teacher should continue to engage in progress monitoring frequently. This is part of the instructional process in any classroom. Formative assessment and progress monitoring are critical in the teaching practices to determine effectiveness. Specific data collection within the small-group setting, data collection within the classroom, and individual data collection samples are appropriate.

SUMMARY

Multiple sources of data are brought together to create a more complete picture of a student. No one piece of data can fully communicate about the student accurately, although any one piece can raise questions or provide important information. The data in Tier 1 include information from the past. Sources such as previous summative assessments, standardized testing results, and grades from prior years provide information to examine. Pre-assessments and screening data also may add to the picture for a more accurate view. During the current school year, while instruction is ongoing, formative assessments and progress monitoring contribute to the information about the student. In some cases, even diagnostics can contribute to data in Tier 1. Together, all of these pieces play a significant role in Tier 1 individually and together as a whole. These data are used to make decisions about instruction and teaching strategies and to determine whether additional supports and services are needed. The data also raise questions, confirm or deny the effectiveness of instruction, or determine approaches to instruction. All of these actions are part of the process of DI and responsive teaching.

QUESTIONS TO CONSIDER

- Describe your personal philosophy that balances the knowledge of the student through personal interactions and the knowledge of the student through data. How has this changed over time?

- What information exists to provide insight into each student before the first meeting with him or her?
- How can multiple sources of previously recorded data assist in planning for the semester? How often does the practice of reflecting on data before planning instruction occur?
- What vehicles exist to help access those data?
- Is there a clear understanding of what the data mean? For example, is there clarity on data that are communicated in raw scores as opposed to percentile scores?
- Is there a resource person accessible to assist with the interpretation of scores and the processing of data in order to create an accurate picture?
- How can technology be used to manage and record data in a way to help other teachers?
- When looking at screening results, is there as much focus on student strengths as there is on student needs?
- What do you do as a teacher when scores from one instrument are vastly different than scores from another instrument? What tools do you use?
- When is there time to discuss student data and have data-based professional conversations?
- How do you find time to collect data about students? Where are these data kept?
- How do you promote students' active engagement in the process of tracking their own data?

6

Tier 1—The Environment

When I was young, I taught myself how to ride a two-wheeled bike. I practiced a few times before I let anyone know I could do it. Once I felt confident, I called my parents and friends outside to show off my new skill. I got on the bike and within 30 seconds wiped out in front of all of them. I had set up a situation with such pressure. It wasn't that I could not ride the bike. I had the skill. It was the factors in and around the performance that held the power to bring me down.

In Tier 1, environmental factors play a significant part in the instruction and supports for students. The environment provides multiple avenues for differentiation to help meet the needs of learners. The environment includes not only the setting but also the supports that are built into the school and classroom structures themselves. The environment can be a support system itself or can produce additional obstacles in efforts for students to be successful. It is both physical and affective factors that create the atmosphere for learning. It is both the weather and the mood of the classroom (Tomlinson, 2003). For instance, a student who is regularly in the presence of high-achieving peers will more likely work to achieve, while a student who is amid unmotivated peers will likely be less motivated. The environment can become an avenue for differentiation by adjusting or altering circumstances related to learning.

The environment goes beyond simply the atmosphere and setting of a classroom. It includes the values, goals, expectations, and attitudes of the culture. It also includes the physical, emotional, social, and motivational components that, as a whole, affect learning. Most important, it includes the relationships between the student, the instruction, and the learning process itself (see Figure 6.1).

Figure 6.1   The Relationships Within the Environment

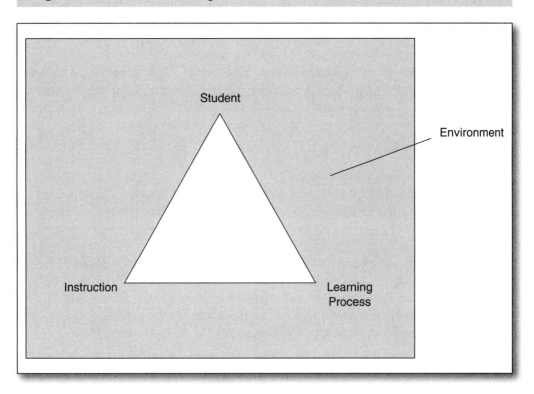

THE SCHOOLWIDE ENVIRONMENT

Jennifer, Aidan, Elijah, and Emily all attend the same school and are in the same first-grade class. Jennifer comes from a broken family in a low-income area. She is raised mostly by her grandmother, who has limited English skills. Jennifer is the oldest of five siblings. Her grandmother shares that she expects Jennifer to take on responsibility to help raise the other four children. She is expected to help with laundry, meal preparation, and watching her younger siblings after school and on weekends. Aidan comes from a large Asian family. He and his family have lived in the United States for six years, since Aidan was an infant. His family devotes all of their resources to Aidan's academic success. They believe he can go to college and help the family by being a successful businessman.

Aidan receives tutoring weekly to maintain his superior grades, and his parents require him to do additional homework each night. Elijah lives near the school in the same home in which his father grew up. He has two older sisters and supportive and involved parents, plays soccer, and is involved with several clubs and activities. He has many friends and is very creative, especially in the area of art. Emily attends the school because there is a gifted class in the school for fourth and fifth graders. Although she is currently in first grade, her parents plan for her to be in that program. As a first grader, she is already aware of different colleges and fields of study. Her parents recently took her to a private psychologist for an IQ test. She has expressed her strong desire to become a doctor of radiology, and her parents encourage this aspiration.

Each of these four students in the same setting will experience school in very different ways. These students need differentiated learning experiences that take into account factors that extend beyond academic abilities. In Tier 1, differentiation occurs through many avenues to include the multiple facets of each student. Academics provide just one avenue. There are many other areas to consider as well. The first is the relationship between the student and the school itself.

The environment of a school plays a significant role for students. The school impacts the community, and the community impacts the school. The school can choose to reflect the same conditions as the community or choose to be different. Tier 1 acknowledges that the school environment plays a role in student performance at the school level as well as at the classroom level. It also acknowledges that factors outside the school impact learning. The values and mission of the school, along with the degree of consensus toward those values, communicate to students about school priorities and expectations. This in turn impacts student motivation and behaviors.

Consistency at the School Level

The first aspect to consider within the school environment is consistency. Consistency does not mean that every student should receive the same thing or be treated the same way. It does not mean that all students have the same expectations. Consistency refers to the frequency with which a student hears the same message. Many schools have adopted a positive behavioral support model in which one behavior program is implemented schoolwide. While this does ensure commonality among teachers and locations in the school, it does not ensure consistency. Different students can receive different messages. The important element is that the message is consistent throughout the day for each student. This section proposes some questions to begin asking in relation to consistency at the school level.

Are clear messages communicated to teachers, students, and the community?

For instance, one school claims that one of its highest values is student safety. This takes on different meanings to different stakeholders, and those meanings may not align with each other. For instance, the principal interprets this to mean orderly, safe learning environments in the classroom and cafeteria. The principal spends time each day in the building reinforcing this value. However, outside the building, there is no supervision or concern for student safety in the parking lot, playground, or surrounding sidewalks. Parents are sent messages about students wearing the appropriate shoes for physical education; however, students can skateboard through the parking lots with no attention paid to them. The crossing guard, however, sees school safety differently and works to ensure safety on the streets and sidewalks. In the name of safety, the crossing guard does not allow students to skateboard across the street. Parents and students are left wondering what student safety really means to different people and wonder how to comply with seemingly inconsistent rules. With all of these interpretations and perspectives, students often see the rules as a game and focus their efforts on trying to figure out the different rules of different people. Without knowing what the value means and how it looks, educators cannot expect students to appropriately comply. Furthermore, without consistency in meaning and interpretation, they cannot expect students to even know *how* to comply.

When we look back at the four students described earlier, we can differentiate the implementation of the rule. This does not mean having different expectations or standards for different students. In the case of attendance, the same expectation is upheld for all students, with the belief that strong attendance leads to higher student achievement. The differentiation can occur in the way that consequences for not complying are developed. It is no secret to students that peers have different home lives from one another and therefore have different reactions to consequences. Students understand that what constitutes a consequence for one student may not be a consequence to another.

The school expectation is that students must walk within the school building at all times and in all settings. The school differentiates the responses of the students who violate or comply with this rule in different ways. Consider these examples: If Jennifer, who helps take care of siblings after school, is running in the cafeteria, she will be required to explain to younger students about the dangers of running in the cafeteria. If a student like Jennifer is rewarded with compliance, she may be allowed to bring siblings with her to an afterschool activity where someone else watches the children. Aidan, who has a highly involved family working to get him ready for college, is the easiest to address. With parents this involved, a phone call to the parents carries more weight than any other action. Elijah, who is very social and active, is also an easier type of student to deal with. His value on being active and socializing can be capitalized on. Taking from him time he would normally spend running with friends serves as a negative consequence, while extra time with friends or in a physical or creative activity is a positive reinforcer.

In this example, the expectation is consistent and yet the consequences, positive and negative, are differentiated. The purpose of consequences in Tier 1 is to support compliance with the core behavioral plan. While each student cannot have individualized plans, common student profiles can be identified and then generic plans developed for each. For instance, in the above example, there are three typical student profiles aligned to different values. One is based on academic success, another on socialization and activity, and a third on outside responsibilities. Most students would fall into one of these categories in which to develop plans based on personal and family values.

Are the school's stated values aligned to the actual
values demonstrated within the school's culture?

In order to have consistency, there must be agreed-upon values that hold true for the populations impacted. Without common values, fractured or inconsistent messages develop. This leads to confusion and mixed messages rather than believing in the common values. The values established by the school must be aligned to the culture of the school. Consistency between the values and the culture must be evident. For instance, a school communicates clearly that improved wellness can be obtained through proper food and drink choices. It communicates this value through the school lunch options offered along with policies related to not allowing sugary snacks, food rewards, or soft drinks in the school. The school has clear consequences for violations of these rules. However, the teachers and administrators have candy jars on their desks and sell candy bars as a school fundraiser. While the value sounds good, it is removed from practice and reality. Values taken from a textbook or handbook rather than developed from within lead to feelings of falseness and superficial statements.

Does the school have a mission statement and set of goals
that demonstrate that the school and community are working together?

The school community is made up of the outside community, so the two are interdependent. The school's goals must align with those of the community for there to be progress. If the goals are not pointed in the same direction, they will divide rather than achieve success. For instance, a school's values are aligned to highest academic achievement. The focus of the school's efforts is to develop the academic skills of students. This includes assigning independent practice assignments for homework.

The community, on the other hand, is well known for having the top football team, and the community values the success of football. This includes weekend tournaments and many practice sessions for teams of all ages. These two values come into conflict when a student is excused from homework to play in a football game or when afternoon classes are canceled on Fridays for pep rallies. The values and messages communicated conflict with each other and negate each.

Do all the members of the school community
agree with the goals and hold them as the highest priority?

Even the most passionately written and clearly stated goals can be ineffective when there is not consensus. Without consensus from all stakeholders, the environment will experience elements of sabotage. For example, a teacher in the school where healthy food choices are a value does not personally believe in controlling what a student eats. In her class, behind closed doors, the teacher allows students to eat candy and often provides small chocolates as an incentive. This undermines the entire effort of the school community and creates an element of competition rather than cooperation. There is an element of dishonesty and a lack of loyalty to the values that the school has established.

Consistency at the Classroom Level

Consistency is so important in relation to differentiated instruction (DI) and Response to Instruction/Intervention (RTI) at the classroom level because of the systematic nature of the two practices. Rather than randomly teaching and providing supports, the instruction and supports are based on student responses and needs. If there is no clarity and consistency in the instruction and supports, there is no way to expect the responses to have any validity. This is also true for behavior. With no consistency of the stimulus, there is no true measure of response. The responses remain random if the instruction and supports are random.

For example, a teacher decides to teach a unit on the topic of rainforests. She starts by showing a video about rainforests, and then the students read in a book about the topic. She allows students to browse the Internet for sites on rainforests, and finally she has them create a poster about rainforests. She spends two weeks on the unit. The next year, when she teaches the unit, she has students read from a textbook, complete an online design activity, and then create a PowerPoint presentation. She wants to know the best method for teaching the topic of rainforests. This teacher cannot use the results from one group of students and compare it to the second group because there were so many random variables.

With regard to DI, the teacher must be clear on what the objectives are before establishing avenues to support struggling learners or challenge high-achieving learners. Unless the teacher is clear about what she wants students to know about rainforests, she cannot adapt learning opportunities. Rather than teaching facts and assigning projects, the teacher must first establish clarity and identify her objective: "Students will determine the different systems of interdependence within a rainforest." Once that is established, she may discuss specific elements from within a rainforest for some students and provide examples of systems within the rainforest for other students to discover their relationships. Once the objective is established, the teacher is able to provide focused activities with different levels of support or challenge.

In another example, a teacher provides manipulatives to students as they explore and learn the concept of multiplication. However, she provides the manipulatives only every few days when she has a planning period just before math class. This equips her with little information to help her determine the effectiveness of providing manipulatives because she hasn't done it consistently. Controls are needed in order to determine fidelity and effectiveness.

More specific to RTI, consistency is critical at Tier 1 because data are studied across grade levels and classrooms. Without consistent sets of data, useful data analysis is not possible. The assessment measures themselves also need to be consistent. It is not helpful to compare sets of scores if the measures are not the same. For instance, if scores are recorded in point values and assessments are compared from year to year, it is important to be sure the point value range is the same for the different assessments.

RTI emphasizes consistency in the classroom under the name of *fidelity*. Fidelity includes implementation of a practice as it was designed as well as consistent implementation. As mentioned earlier, RTI stands on a principle of researched-based practices. This ensures that instruction and supports are based on solid rationale rather than gut feelings or creative brainstorming. Because decisions are made based on the student's response to the research-based instruction and related supports, it is expected that the instruction and supports are consistently implemented as they were designed. This is referred to as *fidelity of implementation*.

In the event that more than 80% of students are unsuccessful with instruction and DI supports, fidelity is examined. The fidelity of implementation of the instructional practice and/or program is reassessed to be sure that instruction was delivered effectively and implemented as designed. The practices involved with checking fidelity are not intended to act as a teacher evaluation. The fidelity-of-implementation check is simply meant to assess how closely aligned the implementation is to the researched method that has proved to be successful. It is an assessment of accuracy, not of teacher ability.

Finally, if the fidelity of implementation is shown to be accurate and there are still not appropriate gains, Tier 1 prompts educators to ask more questions. These questions may be related to the consistency of research of the program itself or the degree to which the research subjects match those receiving instruction. For instance, upon investigation a teacher in a rural, low-income area of Florida may find that the research-based program being used was proved to be effective on a sample of students in urban, high-income settings in New York. This lack of consistency may be a significant factor in effectiveness.

CLARITY

In order to use data to make informed decisions, the objectives established must be clear. Measurements cannot be taken if there is a lack of clarity regarding what is being measured in the first place. Creating clear objectives with defined performance expectations is critical. The objectives must have the following three components that allow all stakeholders to understand the desired outcome as well as understand how close or far actual performance is from the target:

- specificity in description of desired outcome or performance
- a tool for measuring performance
- an expected rate of learning in order to reach mastery

Specificity

It is not uncommon to see classroom rules posted on the walls to communicate what is expected of students. It is also not uncommon to see things such as "Be respectful of others" among these rules. What does that mean? Each teacher in a school may define that in very different ways. Within a classroom, each student also may interpret it differently. It is important when using data to drive instructional and behavioral decisions that the desired performance is specific and clear. Rather than stating, "Be respectful of others," a clearer and more specific objective is "Keep your hands off other people and their belongings." This communicates a clear objective that the desired performance involves not touching any other person or anything belonging to someone else. This specificity allows for measures to be taken. There is a way to clearly identify the desired outcome as present or absent.

Academically, an objective such as "Appreciates various genres of literature" must be restated. Otherwise, how can one tell if a student has achieved the goal or is making progress toward the goal? Instead, the objective can read, "Ranks various genres in preferential order based on experiences with each." The specific desired behavior is essential when assessing the performance and even identifying expectations. Equally important, it communicates to students exactly what is expected of their performance academically and behaviorally.

Performance-Measuring Tools

To determine whether students are successful in achieving learning or behavioral outcomes, there must be a way to measure the initial performance, and the performance changes in relation to the goal. Therefore, it is important to determine how the objective will be measured. For example, if the desired outcome involves students knowing multiplication tables, there must be a tool in place to assess the level of mastery of multiplication tables. Even in this simple example, the importance of specificity is again highlighted. It is not enough to say that the desired outcome is the mastery of the multiplication tables. How many? At what level of accuracy? How fluent does the student need to be? Once mastery is really defined in specific terms, it can be measured. Without defining mastery, a tool for measurement cannot be identified. In this example, mastery may be defined in performance terms as the ability to calculate at least 45 multiplication facts involving factors from 1 to 12 in a one-minute period. Once the goal is clear, an instrument to measure that goal can be sought out. In this case, a tool with 45 or more multiplication facts to complete, along with a timer, would be most appropriate.

In some cases, fluency is not important and therefore does not have to be measured. In the example involving multiplication tables, two aspects need to be measured: level of accuracy and fluency. In many cases, the accuracy defines mastery and fluency is not an important factor. The measurement tool is simply for accuracy of student performance. For example, if the desired learning outcome is to accurately identify nouns within sentences, the tool for measuring must be a set of sentences in which nouns can be identified. The most important aspect of identifying a tool for measurement is its direct reflection of the learning objective. In the nouns example, a tool requiring students to create sentences or identify all sentence parts would be inappropriate. The tool should reflect exactly what the desired outcome is.

Rate of Learning to Reach Mastery

The rate at which a student should be able to master a skill or concept is often set by curriculum or assessment maps. In some cases, the point at which mastery is expected may be determined by teacher judgment. The instructional planning reflects these expectations. For instance, students may be expected to use 10 vocabulary words related to the ecosystem in writing and speaking during a two-week period. This objective specifically states the desired learning outcome and performance expected. It could easily be assumed that the assessment tool will be an exercise that requires students to either speak or write about the specific vocabulary words. This objective also clearly states the point at which mastery is expected. After a two week-period, students are expected to be able to achieve the outcome.

It is critically important to establish a clear target and timeline. RTI considers level of mastery and rate of learning as integral to keeping students from falling through the cracks. If a student is making progress but is doing so at a rate much slower than his or her peers, that student will never catch up to the peers and will continue to fall further behind. RTI focuses not only on students making progress but also on making progress at a rate that will allow them to stay with peers in the learning process.

The chart in Figure 6.2 shows improved performance for an entire group of students; however, it is clear that the struggling student will never catch up with peers at the current rate. Therefore, both progress toward mastery of the learning outcome and the rate at which the progress is made must be considered.

Figure 6.2   Looking at the Rate of Learning and Not Just Progress Alone

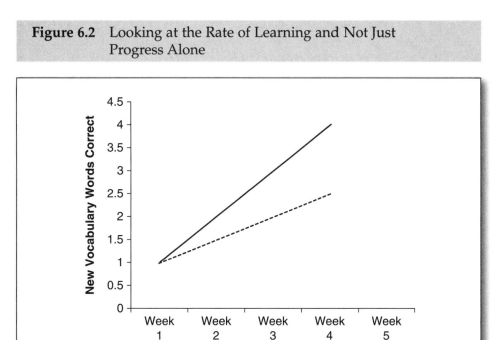

GOAL SETTING

Let's look at Figure 6.2 another way. It indicates that the majority of students in a class are making gains at a faster rate than one of their peers. We assume that the learner at the lower rate is struggling. However, this may not necessarily be the case. While the information in the graph is important, there is one essential element missing from the picture it presents. What is the expectation of the students? Although one student is lagging behind, there is no way to know where any of these students are performing in relation to the expectation. Maybe the expectation for mastery is a score of 2 and all of the students, including the one who appears to be struggling, have already gone far beyond the expectation. On the other hand, maybe after five weeks the learning expectation was a score of 10. In that case, all of the students are performing significantly lower than expectations. Without a clearly established goal, the graph only hints at possible concerns, but the data cannot communicate the whole picture. Therefore, it is important to set goals and communicate these when establishing desired outcomes.

When designing a goal, it is most important to keep in mind the principles stated previously. The goal must be clear, specific, and measurable. There must be a tool for measurement as well as an expected timeline. All of these elements are necessary for a goal to be effective. Because of the different elements involved in goal setting, it is best to design goals as a team. In Tier 1, there are several configurations of appropriate teams. A goal-setting team may consist of any of the following: a classroom teacher, another teacher or teachers from the same grade level who also know the student, teachers from the same content area who are familiar with the content and programs, a person who is adept at managing data, a specialist in the area of concern, the parents, and the student.

INVOLVING STUDENTS IN DI AND RTI AT TIER 1

In Tier 1, it is appropriate to involve the student in the goal setting as well as the monitoring. Research shows that students who actively track their own progress make greater gains than those who do not (Gregory & Kuzmich, 2004). Involving a student in the goal-setting process is powerful and communicates a positive message to him or her. Not only does the process allow the student to know that someone is concerned, it also communicates that there are high expectations for the student despite struggling in an academic area. Another advantage is that the student is then clear about the direction in which he or she is expected to go and can see if he or she is getting there. Teachers who share progress monitoring information notice that students are willing to work harder to improve (Safer & Fleischman, 2005).

SCENARIO

Jon was a second-grade student who was struggling with mathematics. Jon's teacher realized that Jon struggled with number concept, and that was the main reason for his struggles. He did not understand that the number 15 represented a set of 10 and a set of 5. When he did not know how to do a calculation, he had no conceptual understanding to fall back on in order to generate a strategy. Jon's teacher developed a goal to improve his number sense. She created a chart and had Jon track his own progress. Over the course of 12 weeks, Jon's understanding improved. He was able to display his results from his 10 probe quizzes to share with his teacher and parents. When asked about this, Jon said, "I did great! After the second week, see how my line went way up? And then it only dropped once again but that's because I was not really focused. Now look how high the line is."

The teacher did not excuse Jon from doing classwork or homework in his math class. She did not give him any less work than before, but Jon seemed to feel excited about the targeted goal and the tracking of it. He was able to experience success and document it to share with others. He took responsibility as a learner and felt in control as opposed to frustrated. With Jon's ownership, as he improved, his confidence level also went up.

Besides ownership, another advantage to involving the student in the goal setting is a stronger awareness of personal strengths and needs. In the goal-setting process, a student should be able to communicate both areas of strength as well as areas of need. This self-awareness becomes important in self-advocacy and developing independence. Self-advocacy will extend itself to making choices and communicating needs. For instance, a student who knows he struggles to comprehend text as he reads will exercise self-advocacy by requesting an auditory version of the text.

INVOLVING PARENTS IN DI AND RTI AT TIER 1

Parents who are involved with their children's schooling are more likely to increase their own efforts to help their children be successful. A parent who knows what is being learned in school is more likely to seek out reinforcing opportunities outside the school setting that are specific to the learning. Therefore, involving parents in the goal-setting process is also beneficial. Both DI and RTI have shifted the focus from simply the academics to the whole child. This includes what occurs outside the school walls and school day. While many factors outside the school cannot be controlled, these factors are at least acknowledged. Parents play a significant part in a child's academic life and learning, and it is important to involve them whenever possible.

The problem-solving process for an individual at Tier 1 is often done as a case conference or parent-teacher conference. Having the parents and student involved is ideal. The tool shown in Figure 6.3 begins with collection and examination of data to determine if in fact a problem may exist. Once it has been determined that there may be a problem, valuable discussions around each element listed will help identify the source of the problem. Finally, after a hypothesis is made about the problem, action planning is completed. This tool provides a venue for communication

Figure 6.3   Critical Data Processing Questions for Tier 1 Problem
Solving for an Individual

Standard, topic, skill, or concept being examined:

_____

What is the expectation or goal for this standard, topic, skill, or concept?

_____

Define the scope of the problem:

1. How is the student performing in relation to the expectation or goal?

2. How is the student performing in relation to peers in the district?

3. How is the student performing in relation to peers in the school?

4. How is the student performing in relation to peers in grade level?

5. How is the student performing in relation to peers in the class?

6. Are the data consistent across different measures?

Analyze the problem:

Consider each of the following in relation to the concern.

Assessment tool(s) used to measure achievement	
Assessment tool(s) used to measure progress	
Programs implemented	
Prerequisite skills	
Amount of time provided for practice	
Environmental conditions at school and outside	
Student motivation	
Priority communicated by respected people	
Others who may be able to help	

Create a hypothesis:

Why is the problem occurring? Which areas above may be problematic?

What would help this student?

Develop the instruction/intervention design:

Who will implement the plan?	
What actions will be taken?	
How often will the instruction/intervention be provided?	
For how much time will the instruction/intervention be provided?	
For how much time will the instruction/intervention be provided until the plan is reassessed?	

about the various aspects that impact learning and may increase the effectiveness of problem identification and the identification of possible solutions in group discussion.

WHEN LARGE POPULATIONS ARE NOT SUCCESSFUL

So far, discussion has been mostly about two important elements of Tier 1: establishing expectations and differentiating for a struggling learner. Tier 1 requires quality core instruction and a universal behavior plan that includes the practices of differentiation. This differentiation may be in the form of supports or challenges in academics, motivation, socialization, or behavior. The other aspect of Tier 1 involves the expectation that 80% of students can be expected to experience success with quality core instruction and a systematic behavior plan with clear expectations. This quantity of 80% is approximate and is used to guide decision making. It is not a hard and fast rule. However, when a large majority of students are not experiencing success with a quality core curriculum or behavior plan, there are new issues to consider and differentiation needs to be implemented a bit differently. The first reaction is to explore the conditions related to the possible problem. This is done to determine if the lack of success is occurring throughout the entire school, the grade level, or just within a particular class.

SCENARIO

Mr. Jensen taught the concept of multiplication and its relationship to addition for a week. After a week of core instruction, he found that a majority of students still did not understand the desired learning concepts. Mr. Jensen had provided the content in a variety of formats using manipulatives, visuals, and clear systematic instruction. He had also provided multiple opportunities for practice. He differentiated instruction using small-group formats designed to provide scaffolded instruction. This meant his different groups each received different levels of teacher assistance and support. Mr. Jensen needed to include some time on problem solving, so he recruited the assistance of the school-based math coach. Together they examined his students' results and his instructional approaches and practices and determined that the instruction and differentiation had been implemented with fidelity. This would be the first of several issues to consider. Once addressed, more questions related to the curriculum, instruction, learners, and environment must be asked.

In Tier 1, problem-solving questions for large groups of students must look at academic or behavioral performance in relation to other groups. Questions should also consider performance in relation to the expectation. In some cases, the expectation needs to change. More likely, the approaches and environmental factors must be taken into consideration and altered. This is more desirable than lowering expectations. Differentiation allows for the high expectations with differing levels of supports to achieve them. In order to set the stage for differentiation, the problem-solving process must first identify the area in which to provide the adjustments or added supports. This identification is done through questioning various elements.

Tier 1 Questions for Problem Solving for Larger Groups

1. Has the instruction or behavior plan been implemented with fidelity?

2. Has reasonable time been provided for both learning and practice?

3. Has the desired learning objective been examined to determine the subskills required for success? Is there evidence of success of the subskills for most students?

4. Is the lack of success consistent with screening data?

5. Is the problem evident or consistent on an even larger scale (whole school or district)?

6. Have outside factors related to motivational or social issues been considered?

Notice that Questions 1–3 are related to curriculum and instruction. These questions were addressed in Chapter 4. Questions 4 and 5 are related to data and assessment, which were addressed in Chapter 5.

Question 6 relates to the environmental factors that are often overlooked. These areas have different considerations for differentiation than with curriculum and instruction as well as different elements of data collection than typical assessments. Yet these areas are as important as any others in the problem-solving process.

MOTIVATION

When the fidelity of curriculum and instruction has been confirmed as being appropriate through the use of data, student motivation must be considered. Elements related to motivation can often be widespread and may affect the performance of groups of students, in terms of both academic performance and behavior. Therefore, factors related to motivation should be looked at with great care. In practice, these factors are often the most overlooked and yet are sometimes the most obvious of causes for poor performance. For instance, a teacher may be teaching a great unit during the weeks between Thanksgiving and Winter Break. The external distractions may be a major factor in students' ability to focus on the instruction. In this case, differentiation of instruction should include the use of short-term goals with immediate feedback and rewards. It may also include the use of frequent breaks so that students can focus for short periods of time. Another motivational element may include students' lack of value or perceived importance of the learning goals. These factors exist outside the classroom itself and cannot necessarily be controlled; however, they do need to be acknowledged and addressed.

SCENARIO

Mr. Jensen wondered if motivation was an issue. He wondered if the holidays were the cause of his students' lack of achievement. Together with the math coach, he determined that students also might not see the importance of the skills and concepts being taught. The next day Mr. Jensen focused his lessons on the motivation of his students using differentiated strategies. He grouped students by their interests and learning preferences. In these groups they experienced real-world applications for the skills they were learning. One group watched a short online video of a humorous skit on multiplication concepts, with quantities of gifts growing exponentially. Another group spent time on problems that involved sports. A third group examined the learning objectives in terms of cooking through a hands-on project. Each of these groups was able to see the practical application and relevance to their own lives. Mr. Jensen also made another adjustment. Using research related to providing students with breaks, he changed the format of his lessons frequently so that there were no segments more than 20 minutes in length. Mr. Jensen invited the math coach to observe

(Continued)

(Continued)

and collect data. Based on the changes Mr. Jensen had made, they determined that more students were on task for a longer period of time. They also witnessed more students finishing academic work without interruptions related to off-task conversations. After three days, Mr. Jensen assessed his students again and found that they were now able to accurately complete probes related to the desired learning objectives of the unit.

Here are several other factors that Mr. Jensen may have considered:

- relevance to real life
- social factors or events with greater student importance
- amount of time on task demanded to complete the learning activity
- time of day
- students' basic human needs

Mr. Jensen may have considered the last two items if his other strategies had not been successful. He may have created a hypothesis that the students were not experiencing success because of the time during which they worked on math. He may have switched his math class period to a different time of day. Mr. Jensen may have also considered students' basic human needs and identified the source of the problems as a lack of needs being met. For instance, Mr. Jensen may have found that most of his students were not eating breakfast and were sitting hungry in his class. This hunger could greatly impact students' ability to learn.

Differentiation for Motivation and Attention to Human Needs

Motivation may be characteristic of an individual student or may take on the personality of a community. Motivation can be differentiated based on students' values. By appealing to personal values, the teacher can help a student connect with the learning and likely be more apt to attend to the process. Time of day can be differentiated with the use of flexible scheduling. If a group of students typically performs more poorly at the end of each day, it would not make sense to always have math at the end of the day. Changing the schedule occasionally would enable students to focus on the desired learning outcomes for different content areas at times of peak performance.

As mentioned earlier, basic human needs also play a powerful role in learning. Maslow and others tell us that basic needs must be met for a human to seek out new learning or thrive in any area. Generally, basic needs involve food, clothing, and shelter. Without these needs in place, a person is in a state of survival rather than aspiring to thrive at higher levels. The needs of safety and belonging also greatly impact education. Without feeling safe and out of harm's way, a student cannot achieve the great cognitive focus needed for learning without a great deal of maturity and self-discipline. Belonging is also included with the idea of safety as they go hand in hand when considering the needs of humans (Maslow, 1998).

After identifying students' needs, the teacher can provide for those needs through differentiation. The identification is important because not every student has the same needs or is on the same level. It is only after identifying these primary needs that learning priorities can be addressed.

In Tier 1, it is very appropriate to look at group performance across a classroom, school, or district. Using data, educators identify problems for the purpose of making change. Discussions around group data in Tier 1 focus on factors that are common to a group of students. When considering the data, a broad lens must be used first to determine how widespread the concerns need to go. Figure 6.4 provides a tool for conversations and

Figure 6.4 Critical Data Processing Questions for Tier 1 Problem Solving for Groups

Standard, topic, skill, or concept being examined:

_____

What is the expectation or goal for this standard, topic, skill, or concept?

_____

Define the scope of the problem:

1. How many or what percentage of the students across the classroom are considered to be performing below expectations or standards?

2. How many or what percentage of the students across the grade level are considered to be performing below expectations or standards?

3. How many or what percentage of the students across the school are considered to be performing below expectations or standards?

4. How many or what percentage of the students across the district are considered to be performing below expectations or standards?

At what level is there a problem?

Class   Grade   School   District

(Continued)

Figure 6.4 (Continued)

Analyze the problem:

What is currently being done consistently at the level in which there is a problem?

Assessment tool(s) used to measure achievement	
Assessment tool(s) used to measure progress	
Curriculum	
Instructional practices	
Programs implemented	
Prerequisite skills or concepts needed	
Amount of time provided	
Motivation or relevance through students' eyes	
Efforts to improve on the part of educators	
Priority given	
Stakeholders	
Change agents involved	

Create a hypothesis:

Why is the problem occurring? Which areas above may be problematic?

What would help the situation?

Develop the instruction/intervention design:

Who will implement the plan?	
What actions will be taken?	
How often will the instruction/ intervention be provided?	
For how much time will the instruction/ intervention be provided?	
For how much time will the instruction/ intervention be provided until the plan is reassessed?	

Create a follow-up plan:

Next meeting date: Time: Invitees:

professional studies related to problem identification and problem solving. It is important to discuss the elements that all students within a group have in common rather than focus on the variables among the students.

TECHNOLOGY

Technology is clearly the most effective tool in the collection and tracking of data. However, when used meaningfully, technology also plays a significant role in differentiation in Tier 1. It allows one teacher to provide flexible grouping, flexible pacing, multiple approaches, and individualization of instruction. It also provides an avenue for students who are digital natives to work in a format that is comfortable for them. This may alleviate issues of both learning modalities and motivation. Honoring the students' need to use computers to create, collaborate, and problem-solve allows them to communicate in a way that is both natural and effective. Research also shows that students as young as first grade and through middle school who use software for writing outperform students who use pencil and paper (Fisher & Frey, 2001). Embedding technology in instruction must become part of the natural environment in the classroom.

COLLABORATION

Throughout the coverage of Tier 1 over the past three chapters, there has been a strong emphasis placed on the importance of and need for collaboration. DI requires creativity in teaching, and creativity is fostered through collaboration. Flexible grouping is done more easily when teachers are working together. When collaborating with other educators, the learning objectives do not need to be the same for the teachers, but the goal of meeting students' needs in the most effective way possible does need to be a commonality. Discussions regarding strategies and methods for differentiating instruction and approaches to curriculum and behavior plans are most beneficial when several people are involved. Teachers from different areas and levels bring an array of expertise for instruction and working with diverse populations (Murawski, 2005).

When examining data, collaboration is also the most effective approach. In fact, most protocols in the RTI problem-solving process require multiple professionals from different perspectives to come together. Trends and problem identification only occur when looking at data through multiple perspectives and fields. Data must be examined at various levels, starting with the broadest view. Looking at schoolwide data is effective when all stakeholders are involved. Looking at classroom data is effective when examined in relation to other students as well as other classes. Shared data helps both of these things occur. Finally, environmental considerations and examinations are best done through collaboration so that there are multiple perspectives. This provides a broader view and assists with identifying problems and generating possible solutions.

SUMMARY

In addition to curriculum and instruction, environmental factors also play a part in student performance. These factors can have as much of an impact on learning as curriculum and instruction, and in some cases even more. These factors include not only the atmosphere but also the values, goals, and expectations of the school, the teacher, and the class. They also include the emotional, social, and motivational aspects of the student. Together these factors create the relationships between the student, the instruction, and the learning process itself. All of these elements that come together must be considered when providing DI and identifying problems. Responses to these elements make up the significant environmental factors within Tier 1 of RTI. Collaborative effort as a common way of work is necessary to best respond to the diverse student population of today.

QUESTIONS TO CONSIDER

- Where are the similarities between the school and the community in terms of values? Where are the differences?
- What does the school do to reflect community values? What evidence shows this relationship?
- How closely does the school mission statement align with what parents want from a school? What tools or evidence do you use to determine this?
- How do students know behavioral expectations?
- Are student expectations written in a way that is clear and specific? Are they stated positively or negatively? Do they reflect the priorities of the school and the class?
- Are the student learning and behavioral expectations measureable? Is it clear when the expectation is being met, when it is not, and to what degree?
- Are students and parents involved in establishing goals for the students? How could they be more involved?
- How are learning goals established? What is used to measure student performance in relation to the goals?
- How often is the instructional content evaluated in terms of its relevance to the students? What efforts are made to make those connections?
- How is the instructional timeline established? How is it determined how long a particular concept will take to master?
- Are there considerations to routinely assess students' basic human needs? How does the school respond when students' needs are not being met?
- Are there efforts to expand the use of technology so that it is used as a tool for students to communicate, create, and explore?

PART III

Tier 2, Tier 3, and the
Problem-Solving Team

When More Is Needed

7

Tier 2—Instruction and Differentiation

A few years after learning to play golf, I had been doing pretty well until one day when I repeatedly hit every drive off the tee to the far right. The more I hit, the more frustrated I became. After the game I made an appointment with an instructor. I had three sessions with him in which he adjusted my grip, improved my swing, and had me hit several hundred balls toward targets. After those three lessons I was happy to go back on the course again. I experienced a targeted, temporary intervention for my golf game. A Tier 2 service well worth it!

SCENARIO

Michelle is a fifth-grade student. She lives in a comfortable home in a blue-collar neighborhood with her parents, who own their own company and spend most of their time working. She has a younger sister and an older brother. Michelle has struggled throughout her academic years, yet she has never been retained. Her sister and brother are both progressing through school with no significant difficulties. Michelle is very popular with her peers and thrives on attention from other students. In school she often speaks out impulsively during class and does not complete many of her classroom assignments. She has recently been caught cheating on tests and other assignments.

According to assessment results, Michelle has low reading abilities and struggles with comprehension. She does well in math and especially well in art but does poorly in language arts, social studies, and other content areas that rely heavily on reading.

This year, as a fifth grader, Michelle is failing in language arts and is borderline in science and social studies. Her teacher has expressed concerns about her performance. At the beginning of the year, her teacher met with Michelle's parents and established the following supports to help Michelle:

In science and social studies, Michelle is allowed to work with a partner to complete any hands-on activities or projects. She receives all vocabulary ahead of time and test questions are read to her to answer either in writing or orally, dictated to a paraprofessional. Before each test or quiz, Michelle is invited to an afterschool review "club" to prepare for the test. In social studies, Michelle has a CD-ROM version of the textbook.

In reading, Michelle receives support through small-group instruction based on like abilities and needs in a station-rotation system. Her group receives direct instruction focused specifically on reading comprehension strategies. At her independent station Michelle, along with other students, completes drills and practices on the computer using a research-based reading program that involves phonics, vocabulary, and comprehension. She also receives small-group instruction in the classroom to assist with writing skills.

Despite these efforts, Michelle continues to struggle. Her parents are not sure how to help her and have asked if maybe she has a learning disability. With her history of struggling as a learner, and the amounts of supports she has already received, her teacher questions what more could be done. The teacher and parents hold a second conference involving the reading specialist, a remediation teacher, and the guidance counselor.

The teachers present their data showing that Michelle is falling behind her peers at both a significant level and rate in reading and content area vocabulary. The data show that Michelle has not responded significantly to the differentiated supports provided to this point in any of her classes. While others who received extra supports like these have decreased their gaps between performance and goal, Michelle continues to fall further behind her peers and her gap continues to widen. Michelle's parents express a desire to have her tested for a learning disability.

THE NEED FOR TIER 2 SUPPORTS AND SERVICES

The situation with Michelle illustrates the point at which Tier 2 supports and services are considered. This is when a student's needs extend beyond what can be provided through differentiated instruction (DI) within Tier 1. Michelle's teacher has done a wonderful job of providing supports within the general core curriculum. However, additional supports and services must be implemented for Michelle to be successful. These extend beyond the core curriculum and instruction received by the general population of students. Tier 2 provides more time and/or more intensity than Tier 1. It seems this is what Michelle needs. Rather than considering a learning disability and focusing on assigning Michelle with a label, these professionals will focus on what it will take to help Michelle be successful.

Tier 2 is different from Tier 1 in intent. The intent of Tier 2 is to provide short-term interventions to accelerate learning. A student who has fallen behind must learn at a faster rate than peers in order to catch up with the peers. For instance, if a student has fallen behind in multiplication facts and the goal is for students to learn five new facts a week, the student who has fallen behind must learn those five facts along with additional multiplication facts in order to catch up and close the gap. In another example, a student who is gifted has already mastered the learning objective, and little quality learning will occur in the classroom without additional challenges. This student is given additional challenges in order to experience learning gains commensurate with those of his or her peers.

CHARACTERISTICS OF TIER 2

Tier 2 is characterized by more time and more intensity than the supports provided in Tier 1. It is temporary in nature and designed to foster and support success in Tier 1. Tier 2 services are generally provided for six to eight weeks (Lipson & Wixson, 2010). Tier 2 involves small-group targeted instruction with greater intensity than that found in the small-group DI of Tier 1. It is a supplemental approach designed with appropriate materials and instruction based on scientific research and evidence-based decisions. Tier 2 occurs in the general education setting as opposed to the special education setting. However, the intervention is provided in addition to the general education core curriculum. If a student is struggling with mathematics, the student is not removed from math class for the added supports. He or she remains in the class and receives additional math instruction and support at another time as well. Therefore the student receives more math instruction rather than separate or different instruction.

INTERVENTION VS. REMEDIATION

It is important to note at this point that intervention and remediation are not the same. There are significant differences between the two (see Figure 7.1). An intervention is designed to support the instruction and learning process of the core curriculum. Its function is to enhance and accelerate learning related to the Tier 1 core curriculum. Remediation, on the other hand is designed to replace the core curriculum as a long-term service. It slows down the rate of instruction and separates core curriculum from other learning.

Figure 7.1   Intervention vs. Remediation

Intervention	Remediation
Aligned to instruction in the core curriculum	Targeted areas of deficits aligned to goals of areas in need of improvement; often disjointed from other learning experiences
Supports and enhances current learning	Replaces or supports learning in core curriculum
Short-term	Long-term
Accelerates learning gains	Slows the learning process
Designed for a small, select number of students with a specific need	Can be provided for many students who may show general needs for additional practice or reinforcement

Remediation is often removed from the core curriculum with no relevant connections, while interventions are provided within the learning experiences already established in the core curriculum. Remediation is not the same as a Tier 2 intervention. A student may be in the remediation group and not be considered as receiving a Tier 2 service.

IMPLEMENTATION OF TIER 2 SUPPORTS AND SERVICES

Tier 2 is also different in terms of implementation design. The strategies for differentiation are different when providing Tier 2 supports and services, which are determined as needed after reflecting on data that show a lack of appropriate learning gains for a student even after Tier 1 supports and services have been appropriately implemented. For example, remember that Michelle is not progressing satisfactorily even with the Tier 1 supports. She needs the Tier 1 supports that are already in place, but she also needs something more in order to be successful.

Tier 2 is characterized by being temporary in nature. The supports and services are intended to be both effective and efficient. Therefore the intervention itself is approached with the perspective that it will be short lived and may not be practical as a permanent solution. For instance, if a person breaks an ankle, often crutches are provided while the ankle heals. It is not expected that crutches will always be needed. If a person has an ankle problem that will last for a lifetime, solutions other than crutches are most often selected as being more appropriate. The solution, or the intervention, in the case of Tier 2 Response to Instruction/Intervention (RTI), is matched to need as well as timeline.

By nature, Tier 2 is driven by data. Data are most readily applicable to the measurement of skills. For instance, it is easy to measure the number of words a student reads correctly in one minute. It is a simple exercise to establish an aim line for the purpose of determining whether students are reading the number of words that would cause them to be considered proficient. Measures such as these can be compared across peer groups, grade levels, and schools. It is much more difficult to measure conceptual understandings. For instance, measuring students' ability to identify themes and patterns within different genres of literature is not as easy to do. Therefore, Tier 2 tends to focus on the skills needed as a foundation in order to understand the concepts of Tier 1. Reflecting back on the 10 steps of DI discussed in Chapter 2, the steps clearly highlight the importance of attending to skills and concepts differently.

DIFFERENTIATION AT TIER 2

Because Tier 2 is mostly based on skill acquisition, the differentiation involved provides targeted accommodations to support the learning of specific skills. In Chapter 4, suggested accommodations were provided as Tier 1 accommodations. These were fairly global in nature and supported the learning of concepts as well as skills. In Tier 2, the accommodations are specific skill-based, targeted systematic supports. They are also frequently built into the instruction itself rather than being a support, such as providing a highlighter to be used independently by a student. While Tier 2 is characterized by small-group instruction, even within the small group there may be differentiation of instruction.

Environmental Accommodations

If direct, scripted instruction is implemented as a Tier 2 service, the differentiation must take the form of environmental adjustments rather than content or processing. Consider the following examples:

- Adjust the lighting.
- Provide white noise or background noise.
- Eliminate noises or auditory distracters.
- Provide a specific place, posture, or seating arrangement for a student to use for self-control.
- Allow frequent breaks.
- Use physical or positional techniques to anchor ideas in space.
- Provide increased reinforcements or prompts.

If the additional supports and services of Tier 2 lend themselves to flexible approaches and strategies, accommodations may come in the form of changes to instruction, processing, or output. These are different in their specificity from the accommodations provided in the core curriculum of Tier 1. These accommodations are intense and, in many cases, not easily implemented or appropriate for large numbers of students at the same time.

Accommodations to Processing and Output

- Use electronic systems such as a word-processing program.
- Use specific visual cues or organizers targeted toward a skill or behavior.
- Use specialized learning tools.
- Use specially designed manipulatives.
- Provide kinesthetic opportunities within the intervention.
- Allow verbal responses instead of written ones.
- Employ practices that front-load with multiple examples and models.

INSTRUCTIONAL DESIGN FOR TIER 2

When designing any intervention for students in need of Tier 2 supports and services, some critical components must be considered (see Figure 7.2). First, the intervention must be research or evidence based. A research-based program or method is specifically defined by No Child Left Behind as one that has been involved in the application of rigorous, systematic, and objective procedures for the purpose of obtaining reliable information. Evidence-based interventions are those that have documented evidence that is consistent with other research findings, experiences, and proven methods (Rudebusch, 2008). For example, a teacher recognizes a pattern with her students that they are more likely to do poorly on an assessment on Fridays, so she alters her schedule and schedules the assessment for earlier in the week. This is an evidence-based decision. The teacher does not have empirical research to show that students perform more poorly on Fridays, but evidence from her own observation and data collection shows that students consistently score lower on assessments she gives on Fridays as opposed to other days of the week.

A second consideration is that the intervention must be delivered with integrity and fidelity. Fidelity refers to the intervention being delivered in the manner in which it was designed. An intervention must be delivered as designed in order to collect reliable data related to the learning gains of students. Fidelity to the design includes the system or method by which the instruction is delivered, the amount of time in which the student receives the intervention, the frequency with which the student receives the intervention, and the group size in which it is received. True fidelity of implementation also requires instruction that is accurate to the design model and especially a belief by the instructor that the intervention will be effective.

A third consideration has to do with the support provided to the intervention plan itself. This involves providing professional development to

Figure 7.2   Questions for Consideration of Intervention Development

- Is the intervention aligned to the learning need of the student?
- Is the intervention research or evidence based?
- Is the research or evidence based on subjects similar the student?
- Who will deliver the intervention?
- Does the person delivering the intervention believe it is going to be effective?
- Is there professional development or training available to the person delivering the intervention?
- How will fidelity of implementation be assured or checked?
- Are there appropriate materials to use in delivering the intervention?
- How often will the student receive the intervention service?
- How long will the intervention be provided?
- Is there a time during the school day that has been designated for the student to receive the intervention?
- Is there a place designated for the intervention service to be delivered?
- Are all educators who are involved with the students knowledgeable about the intervention?
- How will learning gains be measured?
- How often will learning gains be measured?
- How will learning gains be reported to others?
- When will gains be examined again?

the person delivering the instruction and the appropriate materials and resources that are needed. Another related factor is the provision of space and time in which to provide the service. A wonderful intervention provided in the cafeteria during lunch will have questionable effectiveness.

A fourth consideration involves the length of time that the intervention will be provided and the frequency with which it will occur. There must be a balance when determining how long to provide an intervention. While Tier 2 is designed to be short term, the intervention must be provided for an appropriate period of time to make an impact on student learning. An intervention provided for one week is unlikely to produce significant learning gains. Often behavioral interventions show a decline in desired behaviors before an improvement is seen, so too short a time may not be helpful or accurate. However, one that is provided for a year or even half a year without adjustments would also be inappropriate. Any intervention being provided as a Tier 2 service should be reviewed frequently with data to determine whether progress is being made. Frequency and duration are related to each other and will contribute to the effectiveness of the student progress.

A final consideration related to the development of an intervention is the method used to monitor and report progress. This will be addressed in much more detail in Chapter 8, but it is important to mention here that a plan must be in place for both monitoring and reporting progress. The frequency with which progress is measured and the tool that is used are critical to determining any impact of the intervention. All stakeholders, including the parents and the student, should receive the reports of progress.

STANDARD TREATMENT PROTOCOL INTERVENTIONS

Standard treatment protocol is one approach to interventions. It provides students who are not progressing at acceptable rates with a standard treatment or designated support system. The approach emphasizes interventions that are often scripted and the fidelity of delivery is monitored (Gresham, 2007). This may include a specific program or a set of specific instructional strategies. These are often designed for small-group instruction in a pull-out model. The standard treatment protocol approach uses evidence-based practices and programs that have a high probability of producing learning gains for large numbers of students.

For instance, a school determines that students who are not making appropriate learning gains in comprehension will all use a specific computer program for 20 minutes a day three times a week in addition to the regular reading instruction. Progress will be tracked closely, with the expectation that the students who receive this added support will increase reading comprehension performance. This does not replace a core reading program but instead is offered in addition to the core reading program. The same approach will be used for all struggling students in the area of comprehension, making it a standard protocol.

In a second example, a fourth-grade writing curriculum focuses on learning objectives related to persuasive essays. A group of students has been writing the school newsletter, working on websites, and participating in the school writing club. These students clearly have mastery of the objectives already and will need additional challenge in order to experience learning gains. They receive this challenge in an enrichment program for writing two days a week while other students receive targeted interventions related to areas of need. The instruction in their writing program will be specific, evidence-based instruction designed to increase specific writing skills. This is considered a standard treatment because all students who excel in writing will receive the same intervention.

PROBLEM-SOLVING INTERVENTIONS

Problem-solving interventions are customized interventions for students who need additional supports. These are determined to be appropriate by a problem-solving team, which uses data to drive the intervention. The intervention is systematically designed and based on a match between the student and the need. The selected intervention must have scientifically based research on the effectiveness of the instructional strategy or program or have evidence of being a best practice.

For instance, Mrs. Barnes, a first-grade teacher, requests a team meeting about Carlos. She has data showing that he has not responded to the additional supports she has provided in her classroom through differentiation in Tier 1. Carlos has continued to display repeated behaviors that are off task and distracting to other students. Mrs. Barnes, the behavior specialist, and the guidance counselor meet with Carlos and his mother to develop a plan of action. They first examine the behavior plan Mrs. Barnes has in place for the class, the reward system she has for Carlos, and the data that depict his behavior patterns. The team recognizes that Carlos's behavior declines significantly after the first 20 minutes of any transition. The team believes the behaviors are attention seeking. Therefore, they create a plan for Carlos that includes frequent breaks and reinforcers that provide him with additional positive attention when he performs as desired. They establish a peer support plan as well as a plan for adult positive reinforcement. The group agrees to review the data collected in relation to this plan in four weeks.

Most often, a combination of both standard protocol and problem solving is blended into one model. Many researchers agree that the optimal framework is one in which both models are integrated into one tiered delivery system (Jimerson, Burns, & VanDerHeyden, 2007). The standard protocol approach focuses heavily on instruction and instructional practices. If the response to intervention is poor, the instruction is first checked for implementation with fidelity. On the other hand, the problem-solving approach focuses on the student. If the response to instruction is poor, the attention goes to the student as the source of the problem. In reality, the student and the instruction are interacting as one, so they are actually two elements of one entity.

WHAT DOES A TIER 2 SERVICE LOOK LIKE?

There is no one model specified as an approach to RTI, nor a set descriptor of what Tier 2 should look like. In fact, legislation has been intentionally vague in order to provide flexibility to the model. Most Tier 2 intervention structures have some standardized components set by the local agency, school, or district (Burns & Coolong-Chaffin, 2006). In some cases, especially those in which the standard protocol approach has been adopted, Tier 2 services are implemented as targeted, direct instruction through the use of scripted programs. Problem-solving approaches may also use scripted programs if the team feels they will best serve the intervention purpose. Whether scripted or instructional strategies of best practices, certain factors are common to all Tier 2 services and supports.

Coaching on Specific Strategies

With a Tier 2 support, coaching a student is a main element. This includes use of modeling and think-alouds as well as targeted questioning to guide student thinking. Coaching provides alternative ways of approaching the learning process. For instance, if a student is not proficient with basic math facts, he or she may be coached on using the distributive property to calculate facts in a less traditional way. If a student is experiencing behavioral problems and often loses his or her temper, coaching may be provided in practicing cool-down strategies. When selecting a specific coaching strategy, it is imperative to choose one that has a direct match to the targeted learning skill and that is evidence or research based.

Inclusion of Specific, Targeted Skills With Added Intensity

Tier 2 instruction is designed to be explicit. The need for additional supports or services is reflected through the data, and the data collection is specific in nature. Report card grades or scores from an end-of-unit exam would not be a sufficient source of data to drive Tier 2 services. Although these data are appropriate to consider and are an important factor, they must be targeted to a specific skill or set of skills. This is one clear distinction between Tiers 1 and 2. Tier 1 services provide differentiation for a learner who is struggling or is in need of more challenge of a global nature. The student may be earning poor grades in a content area or achieving perfect scores on all assignments, which indicates the need for additional supports or challenges through differentiation. However, if data collection identifies a specific area of need, generally a skill, Tier 2 services may be considered (see Figure 7.3). These services provide multiple opportunities for repetition, reinforcement, and practice of skills for a struggling learner. For a student who may be gifted or need additional challenge, the specificity comes with increased attention to details or more depth of study. In either case, Tier 2 provides support with greater intensity than what is provided in Tier 1. A significant difference—supported by data as either much higher or lower than peers—in any of the areas shown in Figure 7.3 would prompt consideration of Tier 2 services or supports.

Figure 7.3   Targeted Areas of Supports or Services for Tier 2

Reading	Math	Writing	Behavior
Word-attack skills	Basic operations	Handwriting	Attention seeking
Fluency	Number facts	Spelling	Self-control when frustrated
Comprehension	Place value	Grammar	Handling criticism or failure
Phonemic or phonics skills	Problem solving	Topic development	Emotional outbursts
Vocabulary	Measurement	Organization	Self-injurious behavior
Use of text features	Reading tables and graphs	Sentence structure	Aggression toward peers

Increased Reinforcement and Progress Monitoring Measurements

Tier 2 provides an atmosphere of intensity. Because of their short-term nature and focus on acceleration, Tier 2 services and supports provide more reinforcements to accompany more learning. The reinforcers provided may be embedded in the learning process itself or may be a system of intentional reinforcements, which promote positive outcomes. The increased frequency of data collection is critical to Tier 2. Generally, progress monitoring data are reviewed at least weekly. The actual data collection within a Tier 2 service is best done daily, even when intervention time is not provided. This is so that conditional performance does not occur, meaning that a student only performs well when being tested, rather than consistently. With regard to behavior, data collection should be written in a positive format, gathering data on the desired behavior rather than on the nondesired behavior.

TIER 2 CAUTIONS

The importance of knowing the desired learning outcome cannot be overemphasized. RTI forces this point with its elements of data collection. DI also demands this in order to appropriately provide needed supports or challenges without compromising the curriculum. Earlier in this chapter it was stated that Tier 2 typically focuses on skills. This becomes problematic if there is no intentional, explicit instruction to connect the Tier 2 skills to the conceptual understandings being learned in the core curriculum of Tier 1. While the skills are certainly important and are often foundational requirements, it is important to include a component to transfer the targeted skill to the conceptual learning occurring in the core curriculum.

A second caution relates to commercially designed programs marketed as Tier 2 interventions. Although some of these programs are excellent resources, they must be considered with caution. A Tier 2 commercial program should provide research from independent researchers regarding its effectiveness. It is also important to consider the subjects used in the research in order to compare study populations to the student who may be receiving the service. For example, data obtained from an upper-middle-class student population would not be appropriate when considering interventions for a student in a lower-income inner-city school setting. Another factor to consider is the manageability of the program. Fidelity of implementation is critical, and therefore provisions must be made to ensure that the time, setting, and materials required are available. A final consideration is the specific match between the skills of the program and the needs of the student. Supplemental programs that provide general reviews and practice opportunities of a broad range of skills are not considered Tier 2 services. A program must target explicitly and directly the specific area of need for the match to be successful.

GROUPING

Another characteristic of Tier 2 is the practice of grouping students homogeneously, the purpose of which is to provide targeted instruction to students who all have a similar need. Since it would not be possible to provide individual instruction to every student, grouping is used as an effective way to provide the additional time and/or intensity of a Tier 2 service. Grouping practices within Tier 2 are different from those in Tier 1. In Tier 1, multiple grouping practices may be used as DI practices to include groups based on a common interest or learning profile. In Tier 2, the rationale for grouping arrangements is data that reflect a specific need. This is the case for students who need additional supports to meet expectations as well as those who need additional challenges to make significant learning gains.

SCENARIO

Mr. Turmel is one of five third-grade teachers at his school. He routinely reflects on the data of the students in his class. He looks at his classroom assessments along with the quarterly benchmark assessments used for all third graders in reading and mathematics. He also has access to the standardized testing scores for reading and mathematics from the past year. He has four students who have scored significantly below the rest of his classroom and the rest of the whole grade level on both the benchmark assessments and the standardized testing. Three of these students are identified as English language learners (ELLs) and receive supports from another teacher once a week for their language acquisition needs. However, all four students are not keeping up with the class in mathematics and reading. He has them in a separate reading group and math group for most days of instruction because they need instruction at a slower and lower level than all his other students.

Mr. Turmel requests a meeting with the other third-grade teachers to help him with some problem solving. An administrator, the ELL teacher, and a data coach are also invited. Before the meeting he contacts these students' parents to gain input from their perspectives. He also gathers his documentation related to the curriculum, the instructional materials he most commonly uses, the differentiation strategies he has been providing in class, and the student data. His purpose for this meeting is to develop a collaborative plan to support these four students and accelerate their progress so that they do not continue to fall behind.

At the meeting, Mr. Turmel presents the student data. He shares the attempts he has made to support these students during reading and mathematics. The team agrees that the strategies are research based and appropriate. Mr. Turmel shares graphs depicting data that reflect the students' performance over time, with consistent instruments used for measuring progress. These include the classroom

(Continued)

(Continued)

assessments he has created, assessments from computer programs, and the benchmark assessments. The team asks many questions regarding the curriculum content, foundational skills, and knowledge needed for the studies as well as the results of other students in the class. They discuss the issue of language as a barrier to the learning of three of these students. They ask if there are other ELLs in his class who are experiencing success. Mr. Turmel confirms that there are two other ELLs who are experiencing success with his classroom instruction. The team agrees that these four students need additional support. They confirm that while others are experiencing success with Mr. Turmel's instruction, these four are not. Their challenge is to target the type of support needed, when it will be provided, at what level of intensity, and the frequency and duration of the supports.

In the meeting, it is determined that Mr. Turmel often uses the textbook as a resource along with a computer program designed to provide visual supports for the content of the lessons in reading. This type of instruction is most often delivered prior to any new stories as a way to develop background knowledge. He also uses video clips from the Internet to introduce new concepts in mathematics. The lessons and activities are then completed based on the texts to reinforce the concepts.

Together, Mr. Turmel and the team create a hypothesis that these students need additional services and supports to help them transfer the concepts they see on video to the skills and application in mathematics and reading exercises. The teachers hypothesize that with explicit instruction and a graphic organizer or pictorial representations to connect the video to the skills, these students will be able to comprehend more in both reading and mathematics. The teachers help Mr. Turmel determine four common graphic organizers for each content area that would be used to make explicit connections. He will continue with his small-group instruction using these specific research-based tools. In addition, the administrator will arrange for these students to start the day with the reading coach to receive explicit instruction on vocabulary and application of skills in real-world experiences. They will receive 15 minutes of instruction twice a week for specific areas of reading and twice a week for mathematics. The reading coach agrees to collect data weekly for each content area using a measure designed to assess the specific targeted skills. This will occur for the next four weeks, and the team will then regroup to review the progress. Mr. Turmel offers to speak with the students and parents about this plan.

The previous scenario depicts a typical, simple Tier 2 problem-solving team process. In the standard protocol approach, the team may have a specific instructional program established for students who have a deficit in a particular skill area. If that were the case in Mr. Turmel's school, he may have been able to bring his concerns to the attention of an administrator and the students would simply have joined or received an existing service already being provided somewhere in the school. The example provided is characteristic of Tier 2 because it provides more services with more intensity and time. If this were a Tier 1 service, Mr. Turmel may have provided the supports through differentiation and small-group, targeted instruction. Now, he has recruited the reading coach to assist and is becoming more systematic and intensive with his strategies. As with all tiers of RTI, the intervention is developed to target a specific need as evidenced by data. Mr. Turmel would not randomly begin trying different reading or math strategies learned at a conference and hope for the best. Instead, he identifies systematic, targeted actions that he can take along with additional supports and services to complement his efforts.

IDENTIFYING APPROPRIATE INTERVENTIONS

One of the challenges of the problem-solving model of RTI is in developing interventions. Any intervention must match the specific targeted need as well as be research or evidence based. In practical terms, it must also be affordable in terms of both money and personnel. It must be able to be implemented within a reasonable amount of time, and the resources for the intervention must be in place. With all the requirements of an appropriate intervention, it is easy to see the challenges a problem-solving team may have.

In the areas of reading and mathematics, the first step is to identify the specific area of need. This should target a specific skill. In many cases, the expertise of a coach or department leader will provide some knowledge about commercial programs that meet the desired needs. Many times, textbook publishers will offer an additional set of intervention materials that may align to particular needs. Still, in other cases, research must be done to identify a particular program or methodology. The speech language pathologist is a great resource for knowledge of programs and methods related to phonological awareness, phonics, auditory processing, and language. In terms of behavior, there are multiple publishers that offer teacher guides to behavioral interventions. These are often easy to use and are organized by areas of behavioral concern.

Once an intervention has been named as a possible support, several aspects related to the intervention must also be considered. Figure 7.4 is a tool for guiding questions in the Tier 2 problem-solving process. It considers the rationale for the intervention, the intervention itself, and the implementation of the intervention. It may be used to consider supports and services for students who are not experiencing learning gains either because they are struggling with content or because they are advanced and in need of additional challenge.

Figure 7.4   Guiding Questions for Tier 2 Problem Solving

Name of student(s): _____

Data to examine	Source of data/ measurement tool	When and for how long was data collected?	Are the data consistent over time and other data sources? Yes or No
What data show student performance in relation to the desired learning objective?			
What data show student performance in relation to peers in the grade?			
What data show student performance in relation to peers in the class?			
Other data:			

Analyze the problem:

Consider each of the following in relation to the concern.

Curriculum implemented	
Differentiated instruction provided	
Prerequisite skills	
Consistencies across content areas	
Environmental conditions within and outside the school	
Student motivation	
Parent input	

Create a hypothesis:

Why is the problem occurring? What do the data show as a specific targeted need or area of support?

Develop the instruction/intervention design:

What research- or evidence-based intervention will be provided?	
What materials, space, or scheduling will need to be provided?	
Who will implement the plan?	
What supports will the person implementing the plan receive? From whom?	
How often will the instruction/ intervention be provided?	
How often will progress be monitored? With what tool?	
For how long will the instruction/ intervention be provided?	
Where will the intervention be provided?	
For how long will the instruction/ intervention be provided until the plan is reassessed?	

STUDENTS NEEDING ADDITIONAL CHALLENGE

Several instructional practices can be used in small-group instruction for students who are in need of additional challenge. These students should receive DI in the core curriculum to increase the depth and complexity of the content. In addition, some students may need services and experiences that extend beyond the core curriculum. These Tier 2 services could involve any one or more of the following:

- direct contact with the teacher of gifted and talented students for additional services
- independent study or project
- leadership opportunities in enrichment activities or programs
- accelerated course work opportunities

- dual enrollment in higher-level coursework
- participation in programs or competitions designed for high-level critical and creative thinking

Problem Solving at Tier 2 for Students Needing Additional Challenge

SCENARIO

Mrs. Patsos is a fifth-grade language arts teacher. She has concerns about five students who seem unchallenged in her class. They have achieved straight A's in reading and language arts throughout their academic careers. Mrs. Patsos examines data from their standardized test scores and sees that all of these students are ranked in the top tenth percentile. She then looks at their benchmark assessment test scores from the previous year. Again, they attained perfect or near-perfect scores. Her concerns grow when she looks at the screening instrument she provided at the beginning of the year. The measure shows all of these students as having mastery of most of the language arts curriculum in the first week of the school year.

Mrs. Patsos feels she needs more specific data for these students, so she conferences with each for five minutes and administers some off-level reading passages used for one-minute fluency measures. She includes a comprehension check to ensure that all five of the students understand what they are reading. In all, for each student she collects data from six to eight probes that are designed for specific reading levels.

Mrs. Patsos requests a conference with the guidance counselor, an administrator, a reading coach, and other fifth-grade teachers. At this conference, she presents the data on these students. All are reading fluently more than four years above grade level. She asks the other language arts teachers if they have similar concerns with any of the students in their classes. All the teachers agree that there are a few students in each class who are significantly outperforming their peers. The team agrees that these students are not making significant gains in language arts because they are not highly challenged by the core curriculum. The team also agrees that they would like to see these students receive a more intense program in which they are challenged with material from a higher reading level. This would enable the students to learn strategies for organizing ideas about the content of the material as well as more advanced word study to include higher-level vocabulary. The reading coach shares that she is familiar with a program in which students read and discuss books similar to a book study forum and also enter competitions online for vocabulary. The competitions were included in a recent professional journal on literacy as being effective for meeting the needs of high-level readers.

As a plan is forming, the teachers determine that they will include a total of about 12 fifth graders in the program. The administrator offers to purchase materials that the reading coach would need in order to start this book group for these advanced readers. The reading coach develops a plan for implementation, data collection, and communication with the fifth-grade teachers. She will meet with the students three times each week. She will collect data related to their word-study skills as well as their comprehension of the advanced texts. She will also share all the lessons through the school's electronic posting system so that the teachers will be able to bridge these students' reading to the core curriculum. The team will meet every two weeks to communicate as a group and review data collected in class and in the book group. The teachers agree to discuss this plan with these students and their parents.

COLLABORATION AND FINDING TIME

As each of the examples in this chapter has shown, Tier 2 requires collaboration between many professionals. Due to the intensity, small-group model, and additional time required, the general education curriculum cannot provide Tier 2 supports and services for all student needs in a typical class. There is only so much time in a day and only so many opportunities during the day to provide more supports and services. The problem-solving aspect of Tier 2 also requires collaboration. Groups of professionals together are able to share multiple perspectives and offer different areas of expertise. RTI is founded on a principle that all students are everyone's responsibility. Therefore, collaboration is essential.

One of the ways to find time to provide the intense support of Tier 2 is to share students. If there are five learners with reading fluency issues in Classroom A, there are likely to be four or five more in Classroom B. The teachers from Classrooms A and B can join efforts to provide Tier 2 supports and services. For instance, two days a week, the 10 students who need more intense instruction in reading fluency will report to Teacher A while Teacher B takes the other students for a writing lesson during the first 10 or 15 minutes of instruction. Teacher A provides the targeted instruction for those students during that time. Then all the students go back to their scheduled class and core instruction resumes.

Using before-school time, afterschool time, or lunch periods may be an option for students to receive the additional supports and services needed. Unlike previously funded models that required services to be provided only during the school day, services now can be provided whenever possible. It becomes a matter of providing specifically what the student needs rather than reporting a time or name for the service. There is no one correct method or system that works for all.

Finding enough time in the day has been a challenge to educators since the beginning of the educational system. It is not a new problem. However, to overcome the challenge, educators and schools must collaborate and think creatively about finding the necessary time. Since time cannot be created, solutions must be created instead.

SUMMARY

Tier 2 supports and services are provided for students who need more than what is provided through quality instruction at Tier 1. Tier 2 extends beyond differentiating the core curriculum to include providing more time and/or intensity. While Tier 2 services are considered interventions often thought of as remediation programs, these services can also be designed to meet the needs of high-achieving students in need of additional challenge. Decisions regarding the implementation of Tier 2 supports and services are driven by data that indicate the specific need of the student, which is then matched to an intervention.

Interventions are created by a problem-solving team and may be designed for groups of students with similar profiles or for individual students. All interventions are characterized by frequent progress monitoring, instruction targeting specific skills, and increased frequency and reinforcements. Tier 2 interventions are generally delivered in homogeneous, small-group settings. These interventions are provided in addition to Tier 1 core instruction; they support and enhance the core instruction rather than replace it.

QUESTIONS TO CONSIDER

- What elements of the standard treatment protocol exist? Are they designed to maintain consistency? For ease of scheduling?
- How is fidelity of implementation of the intervention monitored?
- What elements of the problem-solving team approach exist? What people are consistently involved to share their expertise? Are there others who should be included regularly?
- How are interventions selected? How is it determined that they are evidence based or research based?
- What systems of communication currently exist to foster collaboration? How effectively are these systems used? Are there examples that come to mind?
- What supports are in place to provide time for teachers to meet and discuss student needs based on data?
- What personnel are available for consultation during the problem-solving process? Are there others who could be involved that are not currently involved?
- What personnel are available to provide interventions?
- What supports are in place to use creative scheduling as a way to find time? Are there changes that could be made to create more opportunities?

8

Tier 2—Assessment and Problem Solving

Powerful learning occurs in an environment where questions matter.

—Simon (2002, p. 24)

ASSESSMENTS OF TIER 2

Tier 2 is characterized by targeted interventions designed to support or challenge students beyond the core curriculum. Because of that, the interventions are generally focused on the acquisition of specific skills. Being specific, they are not assessed through broad measures such as annual standardized tests. In fact, instruments such as normative achievement tests do not often provide needed information or strong links to appropriate interventions. Instead, interventions are driven by data generated from specific measures of progress or ability for an individual student. Using data, a need for intervention must first be established. *Not all struggling students are in need of supports and services of Tier 2.* One cannot assume that all students performing in the bottom quartile of a class or group need an intervention program. Needs for Tier 2 supports and services are established through a gap analysis. Then, more specific measures provide details related to the targeted need. Diagnostic assessments provide that specific information needed to create an appropriate intervention. Once the intervention is designed and implemented, progress monitoring through regular data collection is essential to determine the effectiveness of the intervention. These practices are the keys to data collection in Tier 2.

Data Collection

Why collect data when student grades from assignments and multiple assessment results from Tier 1 already exist? Collecting data at Tier 2 serves to measure the specific and targeted area of need. Data are collected and viewed from three different aspects. The first is how the student is doing in relation to achievement of the desired objective and in relation to peers. This is done through a process known as gap analysis. The second is the rate of achievement experienced by the student in relation to the objective once an intervention is implemented. This is the progress monitoring process. The third is how a student is doing in relation to other peers also receiving the same intervention. This combines both progress monitoring and gap analysis.

Gap Analysis

The first two objectives of examining data, to determine the difference between a student's performance and the desired objective along with the rate of progress, are both practices in gap analysis. The term *gap analysis* refers to the relationship between a student's performance and both a desired outcome and the performance of peers. Initial data provide information on where a student is performing in relation to an objective. A single assessment measure can indicate the difference. If the desired learning outcome for a skill is 80% mastery, a student is assessed for the purpose of determining percent mastery on that skill. The desired performance level is determined by the expectations of the teacher or, in some cases, the administration. The desired performance level may be 100% if the skill is a critical foundational skill. The percentage may be less if room for error is allowable or if 100% mastery is expected later in the learning process. While a percentage toward complete mastery may be used to calculate a gap, a percentile score cannot be used. A percentile score is not relative to a benchmark and is not criterion referenced. The gap analysis must use scores that are criterion referenced. To identify whether there is a gap, the score from an assessment is compared to the desired outcome. The gap is calculated by dividing the desired outcome score by the actual student performance. A gap of 1.5 or greater is considered significant and provides reason for concern.

The desired learning outcome for a skill is 80%
The student assessed performs at 40%
The gap is determined as follows:

$$80\% \div 40\% = 2.0$$

The gap between the desired outcome and actual performance is 2.0

A second gap analysis considers the relationship between the student's performance and the performance of peers. If all students are performing at relatively the same level, there is no cause for alarm for just that student. If all students are performing well below the expectation, the concern becomes one involving instruction for all of them. Therefore, a second analysis examines the relationship between a particular student's performance and the performance of peers. This is done similarly to the gap analysis comparing student performance to the benchmark.

The desired level of mastery for the learning objective is 100%
The median performance of all students in the class is 90%
A particular student is performing at 60%
The gap is calculated as follows:

$$90\% \div 60\% = 1.5$$

The gap between the student and peers is 1.5

Again, a gap of 1.5 or greater is considered significant and provides reason for concern. If the gap is less than 1.5, the data indicate that a large number of students are similar in their performance. If that is the case, the particular student does not stand out significantly from others. This gap analysis of a student in relation to peers should be completed with peers within a class and grade level when possible. This will give the most accurate picture of a student's need or lack of need for additional supports or services. When there is not a gap evident between students, yet large numbers of students are performing significantly below expectations, the curriculum and instruction provided in Tier 1 must be examined. The core instruction or school/classroom behavioral plan is not meeting the needs of the students.

If there is a significant gap in both the difference between student performance and the expectation in relation to the standards along with a gap between the student performance and that of peers, a need for Tier 2 is established. Once it has been determined that there is reason for concern, a diagnostic assessment may be administered for more detailed information before an intervention plan is developed. In many cases, enough data will exist to provide a venue for questions and suggested supports or services for a Tier 2 intervention.

DIAGNOSTIC MEASURES—IDENTIFYING THE SKILL AREA OF CONCERN

The purpose of a diagnostic assessment is to identify a specific area within the learning or behavior in need of additional support or challenge. Tier 2 provides specific, targeted instruction or support directly provided to a student in an area of need. This type of intensity of an intervention cannot be implemented effectively without a focus or direction. For instance, if a teacher said, "Suzanne needs supports and services because she struggles with reading," more information would be needed to know how or where to begin to help Suzanne. It would be inappropriate to simply enroll Suzanne in a general program that supports or reinforces reading skills and habits globally and call it an intervention. It would be just as inappropriate to spend time coaching Suzanne in phonics skills if nothing specifies that the need is in the area of phonics. Suzanne may be struggling with comprehension but be very proficient in phonics.

Therefore, it is important to identify the specific need in Tier 2 for the purpose of aligning the intervention to that need. Diagnostic measures are the tools to assist the process. They get to the heart of the matter the same way diagnostics in the medical field do. Designing and administering diagnostic assessments take additional time and up-front work, but without doing so, interventions are random and may waste even more time.

There are many commercial diagnostic assessments that are available. Most textbook series include diagnostic assessments in reading and mathematics. When considering the use of these tools, ask the following questions:

- Does this instrument show strengths and weaknesses of specific skills?
- Does this instrument target discrete skills needed for more complex skills?
- Does this instrument provide a probe in such a way that it matches instruction?
- Will this instrument provide new information about student thinking and/or skills?

If the answer to these questions is "yes," the assessment is likely to be worth the time it takes to administer and process the results.

SCENARIO

Mr. Katcher is a fourth-grade teacher. He has four students about whom he is very concerned in mathematics. They have performed poorly in math for the past two years, as is evidenced by report card grades and standardized test scores. All four scored in the bottom quartile on the standardized test in math the previous year. The beginning-of-the-year screening assessment showed that these students were missing several conceptual understandings related to math along with poor computation skills.

Mr. Katcher provides accommodations for these students in the classroom. He also works with them in small-group settings as part of the class routine. These students still consistently perform significantly below the benchmark expectations and their peers. Mr. Katcher has had conferences with the math coach about strategies using the Concrete, Pictorial, and Abstract approach. The math coach has observed the instruction and assures Mr. Katcher that he is providing systematic, clear instruction using best teaching practices. Yet these students are still not experiencing success in math.

While Mr. Katcher identifies basic facts, number concept, and place value as areas of need for these students, he decides to focus on place value and number sense since they are inherent to so many other aspects of mathematics. While there are many models for approaching place value, Mr. Katcher targets the use of manipulatives to support the concept. The concept of place value will include skills of identifying the place value of digits within a number to the hundred thousands, manipulating amounts from one place value to another when appropriate, and comparing numbers.

After determining these skills, Mr. Katcher develops small assessments to measure performance on each distinct step in isolation from the others. For instance, he will present the students with three numbers and they will identify the digit within a specific given place value. The students will also be asked to manipulate quantities into correct place values. For instance, being given 18 objects, students will be expected to exchange 10 of the units for one object that represents 10. Mr. Katcher will administer this assessment to try to identify which elements of the place value create the most difficulties. Following are some of his results:

Skills assessed	Kathy	Jill	Paulie	Yolanda
Writing numbers from oral prompts	3/5	3/5	2/5	3/5
Comparing and ordering similar numbers	4/5	4/5	4/5	4/5
Regrouping amounts into place values	2/5	1/5	3/5	1/5
Identifying place values of given digits	3/5	4/5	4/5	4/5

By breaking down place value skills into discrete parts, Mr. Katcher is able to identify a specific skill in which these students need more intense work. His data clearly show a need for targeted instruction on the skill of regrouping amounts into appropriate place values and some need for intervention on writing numbers from oral prompts.

Mr. Katcher shares this information with the math coach, who presents him with a research-based program of explicit instruction with a component specific to place value. He also reminds Mr. Katcher of the Library of Virtual Manipulatives, where students can use technology to practice place value skills. The four students meet with Mr. Katcher before school two days a week for 20 minutes to receive direct instruction based on research-based strategies using manipulatives to study place value. They also spend up to 10 minutes three times a week on the computer with the program provided by the math coach to receive this Tier 2 intervention. Mr. Katcher will use the assessments he developed as a tool to measure progress as well by readministering like versions every week for eight weeks. Mr. Katcher will also emphasize place value in his daily instruction for these four students as part of his core instruction as a Tier 1 support.

Another approach to creating a diagnostic type of assessment is by breaking down a skill or process into its discrete parts. For instance, if Mr. Katcher was targeting long division, he may assess a student's ability to multiply, subtract, divide, and recognize place values. This practice is the development of curriculum-based measures (CBMs). The objective is to diagnose or pinpoint an area or areas of greatest need for supports or services. Initially, a teacher can use the tool as a diagnostic measure, although CBMs are commonly used for progress monitoring as well.

CURRICULUM-BASED MEASURES

While many effective diagnostic measures are available commercially, there are times when targeted, specific information about a student's abilities cannot be identified through these tools. In those cases, the development of a CBM may be required. Not only is there a great deal of research related to the effectiveness of CBMs when used to inform instructional decisions, but the research spans students of all performance levels (Riccomini & Witzel, 2010). In many instances, assessments tools such as CBMs can be used appropriately for diagnostic purposes as well as progress monitoring at Tier 2. In the previous scenario, Mr. Katcher shows how the tool can serve both purposes. The set of instruments target specific areas of need, but he also is able to use the tool over time to measure progress.

While a CBM can be used for both diagnostic purposes and progress monitoring, many progress monitoring tools are not diagnostic in nature. For example, a one-minute reading assessment for oral reading fluency can be used as a tool for monitoring progress. Over time and repeated administrations, reading fluency can be tracked. But the information gleaned from the measures simply gives a score of the number of words read correctly in one minute. The tool does not target any areas of strength or need within the reading process and provides no information as to the types of errors a student may be making repeatedly. Therefore, while the tool functions as an effective assessment for monitoring progress of fluency, it is in no way diagnostic in nature.

BEHAVIORAL ASSESSMENT

Like CBMs, there are processes used to determine causes of specific behaviors and to target behavioral skill areas that need shaping. In the same way that CBMs break down a skill into its discrete subskills, a task analysis breaks down a behavior to determine the antecedent and reaction to the stimulus. This is most often completed by an outside observer through data collection. For instance, if Mr. Muldoon was having problems with a student who kept interrupting instruction because the student repeatedly called out thoughts, often unrelated to the instruction, during class time, Mr. Muldoon might request that an observer collect data on the student's behavior. That person would observe and record the conditions just prior to the calling out, the environmental conditions in the classroom when the student called out, and the feedback the student received after calling out. These data would be compiled to look for common trends. The data would provide insight for the purpose of creating a hypothesis regarding why the student was calling out inappropriately.

A task analysis may be part of a larger assessment of behavior called a *functional behavioral assessment.* This term refers to a number of different observations, processes, and studies that may be done to understand a specific student behavior. The purpose of any of these data collection processes is the same as the purpose of CBMs. The intent is to determine the specific problem, how often or to what degree the concern is actually a problem, what is causing it, and what intervention can be implemented to improve student performance. Here are some questions to ask related to targeting the undesired behavior to analyze the problem:

- What occurred just before the undesired behavior?
- What occurred immediately after the undesired behavior?
- What environmental conditions were present that allowed for or fostered the undesired behavior?
- What human need was met through this reaction?
- What feedback did the student receive that reinforced the undesired behavior?

After those questions are answered, a hypothesis can likely be developed:

When (situation or stimulus) occurs, the student does (undesired action), which gets him or her (need, desire, or feedback), which in turn reinforces the undesired behavior.

Since student needs cannot be ignored or made to disappear, and the situations that present themselves to the student often cannot be avoided permanently, the objective is to create a desired behavior that still allows the student to receive the reinforcement that is needed or sought. The intervention is designed to reinforce the desirable behavior that replaces the undesirable behavior. The instructional intervention focuses on teaching the student to substitute the desirable behavior for the undesirable one, which allows the student to still have needs met in an appropriate way. Generally, this is done by ensuring sufficient reinforcement of the need when the desired behavior is displayed.

When the student does (desired behavior) instead of the undesired behavior, the student will receive (need, desire, or feedback) as well as additional reinforcement of (specific positive reinforcement to be awarded).

Just as with academic interventions, the development and implementation of behavioral interventions are best done with the collaboration of a special education teacher, a behavior specialist, or another educational professional who understands the principles of behavior. It is easy to mistakenly reinforce an undesired behavior without realizing it. A person with expertise in behavior has the ability to recognize behaviors and reinforcement of behaviors that lead to specific needs being met. Also, like other interventions, the objective is for the student to be able to achieve success and independence. Setting goals for behavior requires looking for instances of the desired behavior. Data must be reported in a positive format, stating what the student should be doing rather than what he or she should not be doing. A behavior specialist can also assist in the creation of a plan to reinforce not only the desired behavior but also a plan to wean the student from depending on the additional reinforcers. The expert in behavior will also be able to help develop a plan for monitoring student progress in relation to the behaviors.

DATA INDICATING MORE CHALLENGE NEEDED FOR GIFTED AND MASTERY-LEVEL LEARNERS

Data are also used as an indicator to determine whether a student needs additional challenge. The goal of education is to foster highest student achievement for all students. In the past, this was interpreted by many to mean that all students should achieve mastery on standards as measured by scoring proficiently on an assessment. However, advocates for the gifted will point out that some students can achieve the standards proficiently before any instruction is provided. In those cases, education is not fostering highest student achievement. These students need additional challenge to grow and reach their potential.

If a student's standardized scores are at the 99th percentile, it can be assumed that the student has likely been limited by the assessment tool and has hit the ceiling of this measurement scale. Another indicator that a student needs additional challenge is results from a screening assessment. A student scoring at the highest levels on these assessments communicates that additional challenge is needed. Finally, the most directly communicated need for additional challenge is through a pre-assessment. If the assessment addresses content to be taught in future lessons and a student demonstrates proficiency on the pre-assessment, there is little need for the upcoming instruction. Any one of these situations points to the need for additional challenge and consideration of Tier 2 supports and services for increased depth, complexity, or acceleration of content.

PROGRESS MONITORING

In Tier 1, progress monitoring assessment tools are used to determine student learning gains over time. They are often quarterly benchmark assessment types of tools that monitor progress toward annual desired learning gains. The progress monitoring is global in nature and functions as a regularly scheduled picture of student improvement over the course of the year. In Tier 2, as with the learning and instruction, progress monitoring takes on more intensity and focus. Generally, assessment measures are administered no less than weekly. More important than the frequency is the regularity. For progress monitoring to be effective, it must be implemented regularly (Brown-Chidsey, Bronaugh, & McGraw, 2009). These measures are used to drive further decisions related to the interventions. These data-driven considerations may include changes to the intervention program itself or changes in the frequency or intensity of the intervention. Progress monitoring data provide the information needed to decide whether changes are needed, reflect the progress toward the goal, and indicate when the goal has been achieved.

Currently, there are many commercially available tools to measure progress in multiple academic skill areas. Most publishers provide instruments to measure progress as a supplemental resource along with the textbook. But progress monitoring tools may also be teacher created. The National Center on Student Progress Monitoring (www.studentprogress. org) provides a great deal of information as well as guidelines for identifying appropriate technical features of any tool used for measuring progress over time. Obviously, essential features of any progress monitoring tools are reliability and validity. The National Center on Response to Intervention (www.rti4success.org) has developed a very helpful Progress Monitoring Tools Chart for Reading and Math that has evaluated common progress monitoring tools for reliability and function.

SCENARIO

Mrs. Walden is a second-grade teacher. She has seen from both her classroom data and CBM assessment data that Patrick is struggling in basic addition and subtraction facts. After administering a diagnostic assessment, Mrs. Walden recognizes that Patrick's conceptual understanding of the relationship of addition and subtraction is lacking as well as his calculation skills. She determines that he needs practice with addition facts in such a way that he will receive instant feedback and corrections. He also needs instruction on the conceptual understandings so that he will have strategies to calculate both addition and subtraction problems using fact families.

During class, Mrs. Walden differentiates her instruction by providing accommodations to Patrick. She allows him to use an addition chart and number counting line when completing independent work. Mrs. Walden provides small-group instruction with flexible grouping based on the performance on the particular objective. In addition, Patrick comes to her classroom for the last 10 minutes of lunch each day to work on a research-based software program

(Continued)

(Continued)

that provides practice and reinforcement of the basic addition and subtraction facts. The program systematically provides addition fact families and provides immediate corrections to any incorrect answers. It also tracks Patrick's progress for both time and accuracy. Twice a week, Mrs. Walden provides small-group tutoring before school with Patrick and three other students who also need instruction on the same skills and concepts. Once a week in the evening, Patrick is tutored in math at an agency where the focus is on both mathematics calculations and concepts. Mrs. Walden has direct communication with the agency providing tutoring, and they collaborate to reinforce concepts of addition, subtraction, and place value.

Although the software program tracks progress each day on Patrick's ability to master his addition and subtraction facts, Mrs. Walden wants to know if she is effective in her added instructional focus with Patrick on the relationship between addition and subtraction. She is concerned that her differentiation in the classroom, along with his outside tutoring and morning meetings that occur twice a week, will not make enough difference for him to catch up to his peers. Mrs. Walden uses a commercially designed progress monitoring tool to track Patrick's performance. The instrument is specific to this relationship and has proven validity and reliability. Because the concept is so critical to future mathematics success, Patrick should have full mastery of this objective. Therefore, the expectation line is set at 100% from the beginning. Figure 8.1 shows Patrick's results from this increased attention to this concept of addition and subtraction.

Figure 8.1   Patrick's Results After Four Weeks

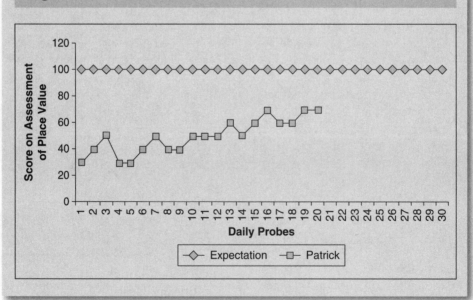

	Probe 1	Probe 2	Probe 3	Probe 4	Probe 5	Probe 6	Probe 7	Probe 8	Probe 9	Probe 10
Expectation	100	100	100	100	100	100	100	100	100	100
Patrick	30	40	50	30	30	40	50	40	40	50

Probe 11	Probe 12	Probe 13	Probe 14	Probe 15	Probe 16	Probe 17	Probe 18	Probe 19	Probe 20
100	100	100	100	100	100	100	100	100	100
50	50	60	50	60	70	60	60	70	70

The data reflect four weeks of targeted instruction. Although Mrs. Walden only provides the targeted intervention once a week, she collects data related to the intervention on a daily basis. The data is collected to establish consistency and reliability, creating an increased confidence level when using the data to make decisions. By collecting the data daily, not only will more data points be generated for greater reliability, the practice will also avoid skewed data from creating conditions in which a student performs to the data. The probe takes less than three minutes to complete, and Patrick can take the assessment independently each day.

Mrs. Walden reflects on the data and wonders if the instruction is effective enough to help Patrick catch up to his peers who are performing close to or at 100% on place value assessments. She brings this information to her data coach and asks:

From this data, can I expect that Patrick will reach full mastery of 100% after six weeks if the intervention remains the same? Will he need additional time or intensity to achieve mastery?

ESTABLISHING AN AIM LINE AND A BEST-FIT LINE

First, the data coach works with Mrs. Walden to create an aim line and a line of best fit for Patrick's progress. Mrs. Walden wants Patrick to achieve 100% mastery on place value. The data coach asks how long this should reasonably take. Mrs. Walden wants Patrick to be at 100% by the end of six weeks. The data coach begins by putting an indicator of 100% at the end of the six weeks or thirty measures. Next, she determines the start of the aim line by looking at the results from the first three probes. She orders the results of the first three probes in numeric order. They are 30, 40, and 50. She takes the median, or middle number, of the three and marks that on the graph. That is the starting point for the aim line, and she connects this to the final point at 100%. In this case, the number is 40, which happened to be the second probe. If the numbers had been 20, 30, and 10, the median and start of the aim line would have been 20 even though it was the result of the first probe. Figure 8.2 shows the aim line and best-fit line for Patrick.

Figure 8.2   Creating an Aim Line and Line of Best Fit

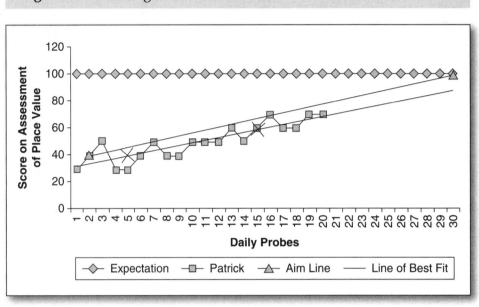

An aim line functions as an indicator to determine how a student is performing in relation to the performance needed to achieve the desired outcome. In Patrick's case, if the expectation were 80%, the aim line would be drawn from 40% to 80%. If the expectation were to be met after 10 weeks of instruction, the aim line would extend over 50 increments (five days each week). The aim line is just what the name conveys—a point at which to aim at any given time over the course of the learning process. It reflects the incremental performances needed to achieve the goal.

Once the aim line is created, Mrs. Walden and the data coach can begin to tackle questions about Patrick's expected performance. For this, the data coach creates a best-fit line, which is used to help predict a projected path based on existing data. This can be done using a computer or through simple calculations. The first step is to divide the graph in half so that the left and right sides have equal points. In this case, the divider would be between the 10th and 11th indicators, leaving 10 probes on each side. The next step is to look at the data on the left side and average all the data points. In this case, the average for the first 10 indicators is 40. The first point of the line of best fit will be at 40, placed midway between the start of the graph and the halfway point. In this case, it will be at Probe 5. The same process is completed for the other side of the graph. In this case, the average for the indicators is 60 and the midway point is at the 15th indicator. The second point of the line of best fit is marked. The two points marked are connected and extended to project future performance.

Steps to Creating a Line of Best Fit

1. Divide the graph in half so that there are equal data points on both sides.

2. Average the data points for the left side of the graph.

3. Plot the average midway between the starting point and the half-way point.

4. Average the data points for the right side of the graph.

5. Plot the average midway between the halfway point and the last data point.

6. Connect these two points and extend the line to the line indicating the goal.

This line tells Mrs. Walden that after six weeks Patrick will be close, but will not have reached the goal of 100% at his current rate of progress. Mrs. Walden needs to make some decisions based on the data. She may decide to extend the intervention for seven weeks, which, according to the trend line, will allow Patrick to reach his goal. She may decide to increase the intensity or time of the intervention to increase Patrick's rate of achievement. These decisions will be based on multiple factors—motivational, environmental, and systems based. It will be important for Mrs. Walden to continue to collect data after making any instructional adjustments. She will use the same graph and indicate the change resulting from the intervention by drawing a vertical line to indicate a break in the consistency of the intervention.

CONFIDENCE IN DATA

How long does progress monitoring at Tier 2 continue? Tier 2 services are designed to be temporary and are often delivered through targeted small-group instruction. Once a trend is recognized, services and supports should be adjusted in relation to the data. For reliability of data to be established, no less than four consistent data points can be considered as reliable (Brown-Chidsey et al., 2009). Statistically speaking, seven points are typically used in order to consider the possibility of an actual trend. If there is a lack of consistency with these points, more than seven indicators may need to be collected. These adjustments may be for the group as a whole or for an individual student.

When using data to predict performance, more data provide more reliability of the data. One hundred scores will produce a more accurate picture than 20. Statistically, 30 pieces of data, collected regularly, produce a dependable level of confidence in making predictions. Therefore, while adjustments to instruction may be made after identifying a trend using seven or more data points, any major decision making should be based on no fewer than 20 data points, with 30 pieces of data being more desirable. If the data are collected for the purpose of driving decisions, there must be a level of confidence, reliability, and statistical relevance of the data.

TIER 2—MONITORING FOR EFFECTIVENESS

A final look at data in Tier 2 helps determine both the effectiveness of instruction as well as consistencies and inconsistencies within and among the group of students receiving an intervention. When providing Tier 2 interventions, there should be a consideration as to how students as a whole are responding to the supports and services. These data can be determined by looking at students receiving the intervention as one picture made up of individual performances. For instance, in the above example, Patrick was receiving additional targeted instruction twice a week with three other students. Mrs. Walden looks at data for the four students compiled on one graph (see Figure 8.3).

The graph provides some important insight. It shows that three of the students are similar in their response to the intervention. It reflects an intervention that may be effective in helping students achieve at higher levels. Interestingly, it shows consistencies as well as inconsistencies in some students' learning: the data suggest an examination of Prompt 4 particularly, where all students showed a decline after having an increase in scores. The graph also shows that there is reason for additional concern for one of the students. It seems that while the other three students are on a

Figure 8.3   Results of Small-Group Intervention

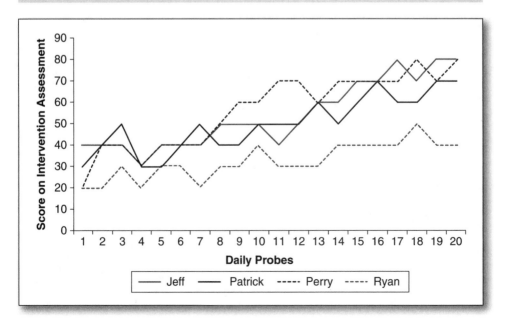

similar track of progress, Ryan has not responded as well. More information will be needed to determine the cause of this. However, because there are consistent data showing that Ryan continues to struggle, this becomes a time to consider supports and services that are more individualized and with more intensity. This is a time to consider Tier 3.

MAINTAINING OR CHANGING SERVICES

If the data show a lack of sufficient progress for a particular student to experience success, the intervention should be increased in intensity or reassessed for a match to the learner and the desired outcome. If data show lack of progress for all students receiving the intervention, the intervention itself should be reassessed for effectiveness. Data should also be examined to look for consistencies in learning gains within the small group and inconsistencies in terms of specific individuals compared with the others in the group.

If the student is showing appropriate progress, the intervention should be maintained until the desired outcome is achieved. Once the data reflect student success in achieving the goal, the student no longer needs Tier 2 services, although that student remains monitored closely in Tier 1 instruction. If the intervention takes on a more permanently needed support for a student who continues to reflect a need for supports and services greater than those provided through Tier 2, Tier 3 services may be considered. Also, if the intervention becomes too difficult to maintain due to its high demand in time or intensity, Tier 3 services should be considered. This practice of using data to determine levels of service includes interventions for high-achieving students needing greater challenge as well. If the student reflects the need for added challenge in a particular topic, unit, or area of study, Tier 2 services may be appropriate. However, if data show that the student demands even more intensity, or if the demand for additional challenge becomes ongoing, Tier 3 should be considered.

SUMMARY

Data-driven decision making becomes more intensive and more critical in Tier 2. There are several perspectives to use when viewing data in Tier 2. A student of concern is first considered in relation to the learning. The process of gap analysis compares student performance to the desired learning outcome. If the gap is significant, the student's performance is then compared to the performance of his or her peers. This creates a picture of the needs of the student in relation to the objective as well as how much more need there is for this particular student than for others.

To determine the specific targeted area of need, diagnostics are administered to provide additional information. These assessments may be commercially available or created by a teacher for a particular skill area. In some cases, these can be created by identifying the specific subskills required for the desired performance. Each subskill is then assessed. This process creates a CBM that can be used as a progress monitoring tool as well. CBMs may be teacher made or commercially made. Like CBMs, behavioral assessments can be created in the same fashion and are known as *task analysis assessments.*

Throughout Tier 2, progress monitoring practices are essential. They are characterized as being frequent, often daily or weekly. These practices should also be regular and consistent throughout the timeline. Progress monitoring assessments provide information about the changes in learning of a student once an intervention has been initiated. The progress monitoring not only reflects any growth in learning but also provides an opportunity to determine the rate of growth and projected achievement. Aim lines and lines of best fit can be established to help educators make adjustments to the intervention in terms of frequency, duration, or intensity. These adjustments should only be made when there is a level of confidence in the data. This requires data collection that is regular, reliable, and valid. Decision making regarding major changes to instruction or services should be based on no fewer than 20 data points. Trends of seven points or more can be determined and provide guidance on adjusting existing supports and services. Progress monitoring can also indicate, to some extent, the effectiveness of the intervention as a whole and when the intervention can be discontinued.

QUESTIONS TO CONSIDER

- As a system what data are used to determine the need for a Tier 2 service?
- How are standards set for the expectation level for a particular skill?
- What diagnostics are used to target specific areas of need?
- How is it determined that the diagnostics are reliable and valid?
- What resources exist to support the creation of curriculum-based measures?
- Are there readily available curriculum-based measures?
- What supports are in place to interpret data once they are collected?
- How often are data reviewed to identify the need for any changes to an intervention?
- How long should a Tier 2 service be implemented before it is either determined to be successful or given consideration for Tier 3?
- What resources are available to support the implementation of Tier 2 services in terms of personnel available to assist in interpreting data and making decisions?
- What challenges exist in collecting and recording progress monitoring data?
- What tools exist to assist in collecting and recording progress monitoring data?
- What Tier 2 services exist for students who need additional challenge?
- How are progress monitoring data collected for students who need additional challenge?

9

Tier 3—Instruction, Assessment, and Problem Solving

Patience and perseverance have a magical effect before which difficulties disappear and obstacles vanish.

—John Quincy Adams

Tier 3 is characterized by intensive interventions provided on a fairly individualized basis. Interventions are not only intensive, but they are also regular and frequent. They are considered longer-term interventions than those in Tier 2. Specialists in the particular area of targeted need often deliver the interventions. In some cases, Tier 3 interventions may require suspension of curriculum in areas outside the targeted intervention area. The types of interventions used in Tier 3 are often more likely to be evidence based since the students who are in need of Tier 3 services are ones who have not responded to more traditional interventions that have already been offered in Tier 1 and Tier 2. Progress monitoring data are collected as often as possible, with efforts focused on identifying what it takes for a student to experience success. Tier 3 often requires more specialized types of assessments and evaluations for the purpose of diagnostic information.

After receiving supports and services in Tier 2, there may be a student whose performance still stands out from the others who are also receiving similar interventions. In the example provided at the end of Chapter 8, the progress monitoring data showed that in the small-group intervention, three of the four students were making gains. One student, Ryan, did not seem to be responding to the intervention. There are many questions that can and should be asked at that point and one of the questions should focus on Tier 3 supports and services. If it is suspected that, in order to be successful, the student needs even more intensive supports and services, the student would be a good candidate for Tier 3.

Once Tier 3 is considered as an option, the Tier 2 data must be reviewed and a problem-solving team assembled to determine if Tier 3 supports and services are appropriate. The team then creates a new action plan to meet the student's needs. Decisions need to be made involving the instruction, the frequency, the duration, and the person assigned to provide these services. These decisions are based on a response to the data.

DETERMINING APPROPRIATENESS OF INCREASING SUPPORT TO TIER 3

The data used to determine if Tier 3 supports and services are appropriate include the progress monitoring of the student compared to the desired learning goal and to peers who are receiving the same intervention. These peers act as a control population. The group data are used to determine how the students as a whole are responding to the intervention. There may be vast differences between them in terms of prior knowledge, experiences, and cultural lifestyles and values. Those differences are factors that should be considered when looking at the data, but the data themselves drive the decision making. For instance, a student who has recently come from a foreign country and struggles with English may be part of a group receiving Tier 2 services. The others in the group may be native to the area, speaking English since birth. The data show that the students in the Tier 2 group are all responding as desired except for the student who struggles with English. The profile of that student does not matter in determining if more supports and services are needed. The critical factor is that the data reflect that this student needs more intensive supports in order to be successful. The student profile helps to guide the development of the plan in an appropriate manner to provide those necessary supports and services.

SCENARIO

According to the data, Ryan's performance has not shown significant improvement even with the Tier 2 intervention. The intervention itself is delivered with fidelity and is effective for the others in the group. Ryan's lack of success prompts new questions about what it will take for him to experience success. The teacher responsible for the Tier 2 intervention asks: What are we going to do for Ryan? Do we continue with the same program and increase the amount of time? Do we consider using a different program for Ryan? If it's a different program, what program should it be? How and when will it be delivered? Who will provide this individualized service?

Ryan's teacher consults with the reading and language strategies specialist, who was formerly a special education teacher and now works with students needing Tier 3 supports and services in the areas of language arts, reading, and acquiring English language skills. Together, the specialist and the teacher look at the data and decide to request a problem-solving team meeting that includes a data specialist, an administrator, and the parents in addition to themselves. At this meeting they will reflect on the data, identify new questions, and determine how to find some new answers.

TIER 3 PROGRESS MONITORING AND DECISION MAKING

Like the other two tiers, Tier 3 also has essential progress monitoring and data collection components. At this level, the data collection involved with progress monitoring is examined with even greater scrutiny. The interpretation of the data becomes critical as the intensity increases. It is imperative in Tier 3 that the data collection is done regularly, consistently, and with accuracy. Reliability and validity are crucial at this stage. Decision making in Tier 3 is more complex than in the other tiers and often involves more professionals. Without strong, clearly communicated data, decision making is much more challenging. When processing information from graphs generated through data collection, it is important to look at the data points in relation to each other as well as each individual point.

TREND DATA AND USING DATA TO CREATE QUESTIONS

When looking at a graph for the purpose of identifying a trend in the learning process, the first step is to look for data items that reflect similarity. These may be based on the frequency with which a particular score occurs or the step change that may be repetitive in the growth pattern. For instance, a student is administered reading fluency assessments for four consecutive weeks. At the conclusion of those four weeks, 20 data points have been recorded to indicate the student's performance (see Figure 9.1). The data show fluctuations but a general increase in performance through the first 13 collections. From the 13th to the 20th collection, the student seems to make little or no gains and scores 43 words per minute six out of eight times. The other two times the student scores 40 and 41 words per minute. From this data, two trends can be extrapolated. The first deals with the inconsistent performance in assessments 1–13. While it looks like this student was making learning gains, those gains need to be questioned. The performance is so inconsistent that it is hard to make sense of where the achievement level really is. It seems as if sometimes the intervention was working while other days it was not. This raises questions about the predictability of the data. The second trend reflects a condition in which the student flatlined in the final probes. What was happening with instruction, learning, and environmental conditions during those times?

In a graph such as the one in Figure 9.1, it is easy to see that using the line of best fit (see Chapter 8) is no longer very helpful. Instead, these data should be used to initiate new questions about the intervention and the student. For instance, what was happening in the learning and instruction during the first 13 probes as compared to the learning and instruction in the remaining probes? The data raise many questions.

Figure 9.1   Questioning Data Inconsistencies

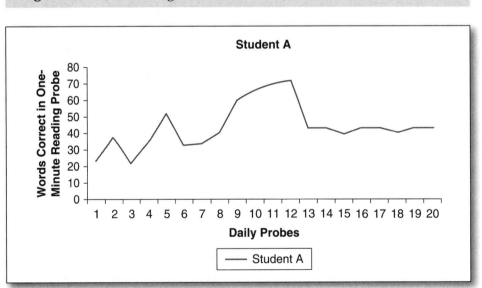

DATA'S ABILITY TO ACCURATELY PREDICT FUTURE PERFORMANCE

When looking at the scores from the first and last probes—24 and 43 words per minute, respectively—it would be a mistake to consider the intervention successful or use it to predict future performances with a strong confidence level despite the apparent improvement. In the examination of the first 13 probes, there is great variability within the scores that create the slope. If we examine those 13 probes as statisticians, we would identify the lowest two scores that occur with consistency across the data points. When these are connected, a line called a *support trend line* or *lower control limit* is created. This shows the bottom line of the graph's framework. In some cases there is a point that is significantly lower than any others in the data collection. That would be considered an outlier and could be ignored. Next, the highest numbers are identified and connected to create a line called the *resistance trend line* or *upper control limit*. Together these two lines frame the data (see Figures 9.2a and 9.2b). The farther apart these two lines are, the more questionability there is about the data's ability to provide information helpful to decision making.

Figure 9.2a   Upper and Lower Control Limits for Reliability of Predictability

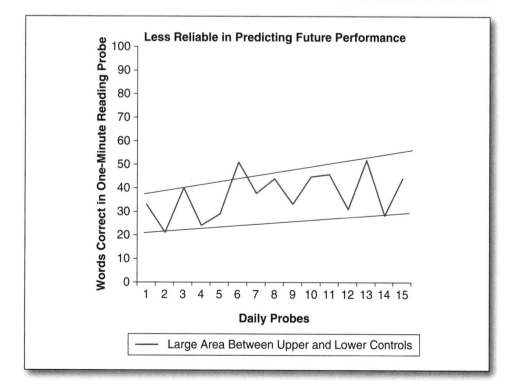

Figure 9.2b   Upper and Lower Control Limits for Reliability of Predictability

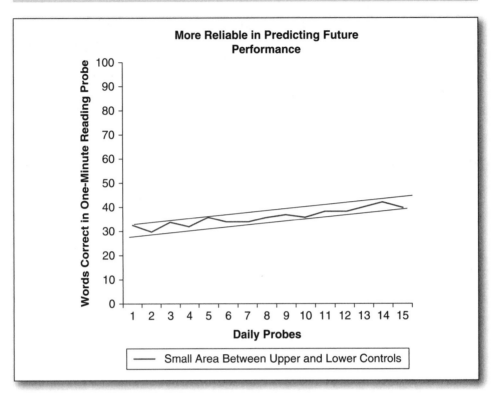

USING DATA TO MAKE DECISIONS—
INTERVENTION OR STUDENT FACTORS?

When using data to make decisions, there are many other factors to consider that go beyond the data and yet are prompted by the data. A student who has drastic fluctuations in performance shows the ability to achieve at certain times and not at others. The question this data prompts is: What conditions are present when the student achieves with high success, and what conditions are present or absent when performance data is low? In these cases, the student and his or her relationship to the instruction and learning should be examined more closely once it has been established that the intervention has been delivered with fidelity. The issues here point to the student and environment as opposed to the intervention itself (see Figure 9.3). It seems that the intervention has the potential to be effective because there are times when the response was positive. However, the conditions outside the intervention itself seem to be a major factor in terms of the intervention's effectiveness. On the other hand, when there is small difference between the upper and lower control limits, the intervention itself should be the focus of discussion. This narrow margin indicates an intervention that is clearly working or clearly in need of change (see Figure 9.4).

Figure 9.3   Data Indicating Performance Likely to be Indicative of an Environmental or Motivational, Student-Centered Issue

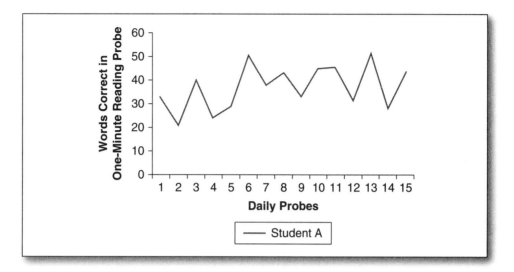

Figure 9.4   Data Indicating Performance Likely to be Indicative of the Effectiveness of an Intervention

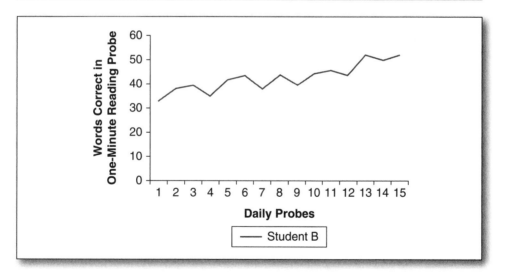

Results such as those in Figures 9.3 and 9.4 raise different questions. In Figure 9.3, the data are inconsistent. Questions generated from this graph should include the following:

- Is the intervention being delivered with fidelity?
- Is the student motivated to achieve?
- What conditions exist on the days when scores were the highest? The lowest?

In Figure 9.4, questions center more around the intervention itself and its match to the learner if progress is not at a desirable rate and level:

- Is the intervention being implemented with fidelity?
- Is the intervention research based or evidence based?
- Is the population in the research group similar to the learner?
- What other interventions might be considered?

These different interpretations of and questions about the data can be used in the decision-making process. When considering making changes to the level of intensity of a Tier 2 intervention and increasing it to a Tier 3 intervention (see Figure 9.5), the data provide insight as to the focus of the increased intensity. We can sometimes use the data to predict future performance as well as to determine the likely area of adjustments needed. It is important to also note that when an intervention is first implemented, especially a behavioral intervention, it is not uncommon for the performance to first deteriorate rather than improve immediately. Questions and discussions should take this into account when using the data for decision making.

Figure 9.5   Considerations for Moving From Tier 2 to Tier 3
Supports and Services

Student Name: _____ Date: _____

Targeted area in Tier 2: _____

Instructional materials used: _____

Instructional strategies used: _____

How often each week (frequency): _____

How long for each intervention session (duration): _____

Supports provided by (person): _____

- Has the student had the opportunity to learn in the core instruction?
- Is the Tier 2 instructional program or material research or evidence based, and has it been implemented with fidelity?
- What evidence reflects that?
- What accommodations or supports have been provided during the intervention session?
- How often have data been collected?
- Has there been any evidence of a positive response (high performance) by the student at any time? *The key here is the individual responses, not necessarily successfully meeting the desired level of achievement.*
- Has there been an indicator of a positive response by peers receiving the same intervention?

- Is the trend reliable for predictability (small area between upper and lower control limits)?
- What differences exist between the student and peers receiving the same intervention?

Considerations	Student	Peers
Background knowledge, prior experiences, foundational skills		
Social or emotional conditions		
Motivation		
Aptitude		
Known disability or processing deficit		

- Do the data seem to reflect an issue with programming or student learning? *Programming issues are often reflected by a flat line on graphed data. Student learning issues are often reflected by inconsistent performance data. For behavioral issues, look at student learning considerations.*

If the program is the focus:	If the student learning is the focus:
Consider:	Consider:
• The same program with more time	• Are there obvious obstacles the student faces, such as limited English skills or lack of background knowledge?
Is there evidence or research that says more time can produce more positive results? Is that research or evidence based on a profile similar to that of the student of concern?	• What occurred during high points to foster achievement?
• A different program than what is used in Tiers 1 and 2	• What does it take to provide those supports or conditions for more regular achievement?
What gives a different program more potential to meet the learner's needs? Is there reason to think a different program will provide a better fit?	*Is this reasonable in Tier 2, or does it require the greater supports and services of Tier 3?*

(Continued)

Figure 9.5 (Continued)

If the program is the focus:	If the student learning is the focus:
	• Is there more information needed about the student's learning and thinking processes? What questions need to be answered?
	What evaluations or assessments can provide that information?

Supports or services needed:	How often:
Where:	What time during the day:
By whom:	

Progress monitoring will be collected through the use of:

Data and information will be reviewed on:

PROBLEM-SOLVING TEAM MEMBERS IN TIER 3

The team involved in this problem-solving process may be different from the team involved at Tiers 1 and 2. The problem solving involved in Tiers 1 and 2 usually involves the grade-level teachers along with parents, a content or behavior specialist, a teacher of gifted students, a person who is proficient with interpreting data, and an administrator or guidance counselor. The problems are often ones that can be addressed through collaboration of educators who commonly work together. Because of the increased intensity of Tier 3 supports and services, there is often a need for increased specialization. These teams often include those from the Tier 2 team as well as possibly a special education teacher, a speech language therapist, an occupational therapist, a psychologist, and/or a specialist in the area of concern.

If the team decides that more information from additional evaluations or assessments is needed, the team should still move forward by creating a new action plan for the student. There is no point maintaining a Tier 2 intervention if there is clear evidence that it is not working. In the case where more information is needed, the team should increase the intervention to a

Tier 3 service rather than wait for results of assessments and evaluations. The plan can later be adjusted once that information is obtained.

TIER 3 AND SPECIAL EDUCATION

Often, Tier 3 supports and services and special education supports and services are mistaken as one and the same. But a student can receive Tier 3 supports and services without any involvement of special education. Tier 3 provides an intervention with more individualized intensity. If the student experiences success at a rate that will allow him or her to perform within the peer norms with these more intensive services, there is no need for special education. Unless there is more information needed regarding the student thinking and learning processes, psychological evaluations may not be needed. Using the template from Figure 9.5, it is clear that a student may experience a lack of sufficient success due to issues with the instructional methods or materials of the program. In such a case, the student may receive Tier 3 services with no need for any evaluations of intelligence or thinking processes.

However, the team may decide they want more information to match the student needs to a support or service. Often more information is needed because there are very few students who should reflect a need for this type of individualized supports and services. It is expected that most students will respond to the Tier 2 interventions. Therefore, there are usually glaring questions about why a student did not respond favorably while the others in the same situation did. This additional information may include a home study, a student interview, a formal functional behavioral assessment, or an evaluation from a psychologist. The information is not obtained for the purpose of classifying the student for a special education program but is used instead for answering questions and making decisions that will aid in student success. The psychological evaluation could, in fact, provide information and scores that then qualify the student for services and supports through special education programs, but that is an outcome of gathering information and not the sole purpose of the testing. The intent is to determine the difference between the student and peers who are responding to instruction and interventions. Once that difference has been determined, a plan to address it can be developed.

TIER 3 FOR GIFTED LEARNERS

In the case of gifted learners, or those who have excelled beyond the expectations, data can also show a need for more intensity of services. For example, a group of students in an advanced writing course is provided with additional course rigor in writing. One student consistently demonstrates superior performance compared to the other students. Even among the top students, this student still stands out. When looking at the data, it is apparent that the student has flatlined at the top of the performance level chart, which reflects a need for a more intensive challenge than the others in the class need. The student may be provided with a mentor who will challenge him or her through professional writing experiences, opportunities to write in different styles or voices, or even opportunities to formally publish work. Like all Tier 3 services, the design for implementation is individualized and specific to the needs of the individual student. Placing this student into a high-performing math class may provide challenge but not necessarily in the area in which the student reflects the need for more challenge. The intervention of more challenge must still be matched to the learner.

FINDING TIME AND COLLABORATING

One of the greatest challenges associated with implementing Tier 3 services is finding time to provide the service. This challenge involves both time within the student's schedule as well as time for a professional to provide the appropriate intervention. There is only so much time in a day. It cannot be expected that the educational system will change to create more time to assist with the implementation of Response to Instruction/Intervention (RTI) or differentiated instructional strategies. All that can be done is to use the available time as wisely and systematically as possible.

There is also an increased need for collaboration with outside agencies and programs that interact with students in their lives outside of the school day and beyond the walls of the school building. It is becoming essential to work with before- and afterschool programs, private tutoring companies, and parents in order to effectively develop successful learners. While it was once considered an outstanding practice to collaborate with organizations and supports outside of the school, it now needs to become common practice. Before- and afterschool programs will be needed to support and reinforce learning efforts. It would be rare to find a before- or afterschool program or agency that would not be receptive to collaborating with the school, but it is up to the educators to extend the invitation. Extended-day programs, organized athletic programs, and various civic groups within a community are all working toward developing successful citizens. When the school and these outside organizations collaborate, the combined efforts will carry students much further than each of the fragmented efforts can.

In other cases, Tier 3 services may require the suspension of curriculum that is not in the area of concern. For instance, a student who is in need of Tier 3 supports and services in reading may have to suspend content area such as social studies in order to receive the services. The reading instruction may be provided using social studies content and topics to compensate for this loss. However, it would not be appropriate for a student struggling in reading to have a reading class suspended in order to receive Tier 3 supports for reading. The student needs more, not fewer, supports and services in this area. However, these decisions must be made with caution. If a student struggles to perform a skill and is made to work on that skill for long periods of time, it is likely that there will be great amounts of frustration and distaste for the skill. For instance, if a person does not like jogging and is not good at it, making the person jog all day will not likely result in that person developing a love of jogging. The student who struggles in school will be even more turned off to learning if all that is provided are opportunities to struggle. Therefore, there needs to be a balance between the intervention and opportunities to perform skills in which there is competence.

Another challenge involves finding time for personnel to provide these intensive interventions. This challenge may result in a new examination of the way personnel function within a school. In the past, teachers had roles in which they were responsible for the students only while the students were sitting in their classroom. When students were not in the classroom, the teachers were not responsible. If a student was not on a teacher's roster, the teacher felt no sense of responsibility for that student. Traditionally, there have also been very specific roles for special education teachers. Their job was to work with students who were identified as having special needs. RTI blurs the lines of responsibility. All students are everyone's responsibility. The special education teacher who has expertise in specific learning strategies may become a learning strategies specialist and provide interventions for many students, not just those identified as being included in special education programs. The general education teacher may also need to broaden the scope of work to function collaboratively with other teachers from the same grade level and share responsibility for providing a targeted intervention. A second-grade math teacher may provide math interventions to a third- or fourth-grade student if appropriate. This demand for collaboration is no longer one of luxury or choice. It is one of need and survival. Educators must work together to take responsibility for all students, and they must reach out to other resources to help meet these students' needs.

SUMMARY

Tier 3 services and supports are considered when a student is not experiencing success from the supports and services provided in Tier 2 while others receiving the same intervention are experiencing success at the desired levels and rate. The differentiated instruction of Tier 3 is individualized and specific to the student's need. The intervention is generally longer in duration than in Tier 3 and is designed to support success in Tiers 1 and 2. All decisions regarding the need for Tier 3, as well as the intervention within Tier 3, are driven by data. An in-depth look at data can provide insight regarding abilities to predict future performance and the area of focus for a different intervention if one is needed.

Tier 3 demands more time, which in turn demands more collaboration. It requires educators to reassess the roles that they play as educators and school ambassadors. They cannot make more time, so they must make more allies. The roles of educators must be reassessed also to assure that professionals with specific knowledge and expertise are used in the most effective way possible for all students. While Tier 3 is individualized, it is not necessarily part of the special education program. In fact, Tier 3 may involve some students who are exceedingly high-achieving or gifted as well. These students also have unique needs that must be met so that they can reach their highest potential.

QUESTIONS TO CONSIDER

- What evidence do you see that suggests that the roles of professionals within the educational setting need to be reassessed?
- What has been done to restructure professionals' roles to meet the needs of more students?
- What potential has remained underutilized in meeting the needs of students who have significant needs for additional supports and services?
- What policies or practices are in place for the suspension of courses so that a student has time to receive an intensive intervention within the school day?
- What roles in the school allow for decision making with regard to the schedules of students and professionals who can provide services?
- What efforts have been made to reach out to outside resources and organizations to assist in supporting student learning?
- What role does psychological testing have in Tier 3?
- How do data guide instructional program decision making at Tier 3? Are these decisions individualized or part of a standard protocol?
- What obstacles exist in providing individualized services for Tier 3? What efforts are being made to overcome these?
- What is done to enable high-achieving and gifted students to go beyond other high-achieving and gifted students as a Tier 3 service?

10

The Problem-Solving Team

To be willing and able to see with your own eyes and through another's eyes is the gift of wisdom. When we allow ourselves to be open to other perspectives and really see and listen, while contributing our own valuable insight, we know the real meaning of being a team.

At each level, the problem-solving team provides a forum in which to address student performance concerns. The problem-solving teams at each level have different purposes and are, in many cases, composed of different people. But the functioning of each team centers around data-driven decision making, and the goal of every team is to identify what supports and services a student needs in order to be successful. This is done through the problem-solving team's supports and its efforts to interpret data. Even when evaluations and additional assessments are administered, they are done with the intention of providing information related to what is different about the student that is hindering success so that the learning obstacle can be overcome. This is a very proactive and optimistic approach. While the problem-solving process often follows specific procedures and uses established forms, it is important to remember that problem solving is a thought process and not just a forms process.

At each level, the problem-solving team's purpose is to assist in solving problems related to best meeting the needs of students not responding to the typical instruction being provided. Therefore, the team must examine data and determine and create an intervention plan. This requires trust and collaboration. The team must consist of people with expertise in multiple areas so that there are many perspectives. These members are people with expertise in curriculum and instruction, someone with expertise in interventions and support strategies, someone who can interpret and manipulate data from multiple sources, and people who have knowledge of the specific student being discussed. An expert such as a speech and language pathologist may look at a problem with phonics differently than a general education teacher would, and both may see things differently than would a teacher with expertise in processing issues related to a disability. The parent will also have a unique and valuable perspective as well.

The problem-solving process involves using data to create interventions that are developed through research- or evidence-based strategies to determine how to best serve a student. The data reflect the student needs. This drives the decision-making process. The problem-solving team also considers all the factors that may influence the supports and services being provided or suggested (see Figure 10.1).

Figure 10.1   The Problem-Solving Process for Determining Interventions

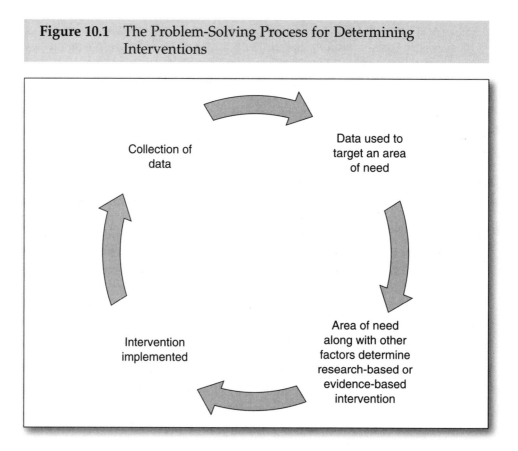

Collection of
data

Data used to
target an area
of need

Area of need
along with other
factors determine
research-based or
evidence-based
intervention

Intervention
implemented

TIER 1 PROBLEM SOLVING

Whenever a teacher has a concern about a student, the teacher has the responsibility of reacting to that concern. The reaction includes collecting data and examining factors related to the concern. If the concern is related to a lack of academic success, progress, or appropriate behavior, data are collected to see how the student is performing in relation to his or her peers. Considerations are given to identifying the curriculum being implemented, the teaching format, the environment of the classroom and location of the student, and any other factors that may be influencing student performance. These influences may exist within or outside of the school.

Instructionally, the teacher provides differentiated instructional strategies such as reteaching and guided practice as well as small-group instruction specific to the student's needs. The teacher also collects data in that guided small-group instruction to identify how the student is performing in comparison to the other students receiving the same small-group instruction. The teacher uses any previously collected data along with ongoing progress monitoring data to track student progress.

At Tier 1, the problem-solving team can function as a teacher assistance team. The teacher is provided with a forum in which to express concern about a student to other stakeholders. These stakeholders may include other teachers, possibly a guidance counselor, and the student's parents. This collaboration allows the teacher to determine if the problem is isolated to a classroom, subject area, or particular event in the student's life. Through communication with other stakeholders or peer teachers at this stage, the door is open for shared responsibility for increasing student performance. Teachers may pool efforts to support the student along with other students with the same need. This is all part of the problem-solving process at Tier 1.

Another responsibility of a Tier 1 problem-solving team is to examine and interpret systemwide data. The team looks at data across the district, school, or grade level to identify areas of strength and weakness as a whole. In many cases, standardized test results are examined and disaggregated for the purpose of setting goals. A school may examine behavior in relation to referrals to determine the effectiveness of the schoolwide behavioral plan. It may also look at specific grade levels to see if there are discrepancies between the levels in an area of performance. The problem-solving team brings together experts for the purpose of data analysis.

TIER 2 PROBLEM SOLVING

If the student is unsuccessful despite the additional supports being implemented through differentiated instruction, the problem-solving team meets to determine what can be done to increase the student performance and support achievement at an appropriate level and pace. At this point, it may be determined that the student's needs go beyond what is being provided through the Tier 1 differentiated instruction. At Tier 2, the problem-solving team may be made up of the student's teachers, past teachers from different grade levels, a specialist in the content area, a guidance counselor or administrator, and, of course, the parents.

It may also be determined that more information is needed to identify a specific area to target. In this case, diagnostic testing may be considered. The identification of a specific problem will direct the targeted intensive supports the student needs in order to achieve success. These diagnostics may be in the form of testing or a review of existing records. The data collected should also include student input. The problem-solving team may be utilized here if the teacher is struggling to identify a targeted area of need. In many cases, the team will be able to determine, through new and past data, the most significant need for support. As the targeted area of need is identified, collaboration is necessary to provide the targeted supports. For instance, if the data indicate that a student is in need of more instruction on identifying the main idea from details for increased comprehension, the student should receive supports specifically matched to that need. This would take place in small-group instruction with other peers who have the same need. An intervention this specific will often require flexible scheduling and grouping, possibly spanning multiple classrooms to provide the student the support he or she needs. This all becomes part of the role of the problem-solving team at Tier 2.

TIER 3 PROBLEM SOLVING

In some instances, a student receiving an intervention at Tier 2 will still not experience the desired level or rate of performance. Again, a problem-solving team meets to identify why the student is not making the progress hoped for with the intervention. By the time it gets to this level, there have been problem-solving meetings at both Tiers 1 and 2. Now there is a need for more specialized expertise to identify what is hindering the student from making the progress that peers are experiencing with the same supports and services. Therefore, the problem-solving team now involves the grade-level teachers and teachers of the content area, educators with specific areas of expertise such as a reading or math specialist, a special education teacher, a behavior specialist or a speech and language pathologist, a person with expertise in examining data, an evaluation specialist such as a psychologist, a guidance counselor or administrator, and, of course, the parents. The student may also play an important role in the process when appropriate. This group becomes the Tier 3 problem-solving team.

PROBLEM SOLVING VS. REFERRAL PROCESS

The Tier 3 problem-solving team meeting is different from traditional meetings designed for referral for evaluation for special education programs. It does not necessarily replace those meetings, because the problem-solving team meetings at Tier 3 are designed for an entirely different purpose.

Referral process meetings are designed to initiate compliance procedures related to the testing and eligibility of a student in a special needs program. The referral team consists of experts on compliance, evaluation, and special education policies and procedures. The goal of this team is to administer evaluations. The purpose of the evaluation is to determine whether the student qualifies for special education services. Often one member of the team, a psychologist, determines the appropriate evaluation to be administered. Those results are reported back to the team for discussion about the scores.

The problem-solving team, on the other hand, is designed to gather and process information and data for the purpose of creating supports and services for a student in need. The problem-solving team may suggest that the student be referred for testing by a psychologist so that the team has more information to help guide the problem-solving process and identify the supports the student needs. The need for an evaluation is a team decision rather than one made by rules or a single person. In some cases, the testing will reveal characteristics of a disability or provide information that does in fact qualify the student for special education services. Even after that evaluation process is done, the problem-solving team must still determine the supports and services that the student needs in order to experience achievement at an appropriate level and rate of success with appropriate behaviors. The information gained as a result of this additional testing helps identify and drive an intervention that offers more appropriate ways to provide supports to a student. The focus of the problem-solving team is to answer questions about what to do with the information from the evaluation rather than focusing on the evaluation as a last step.

One of the strengths of the Response to Instruction/Intervention (RTI) process is that the framework provides a systematic process for determining interventions and decision making. The RTI problem-solving process is driven by data and remains consistent at all tiers. This allows for structure and increased reliability. Figure 10.2 identifies the steps of problem solving implemented at all three tiers of services and supports.

Figure 10.2   Steps of Problem Solving

1. Identify the specific targeted problem area.
   - Must be based on data sources
   - Must be specific, measureable, and shown to hinder performance

2. Ensure that the quality core curriculum is being administered with fidelity and differentiated strategies that include accommodations.

3. Identify the gap between learner and desired outcome.

4. Identify the gap between learner and peers.

(Continued)

Figure 10.2 (Continued)

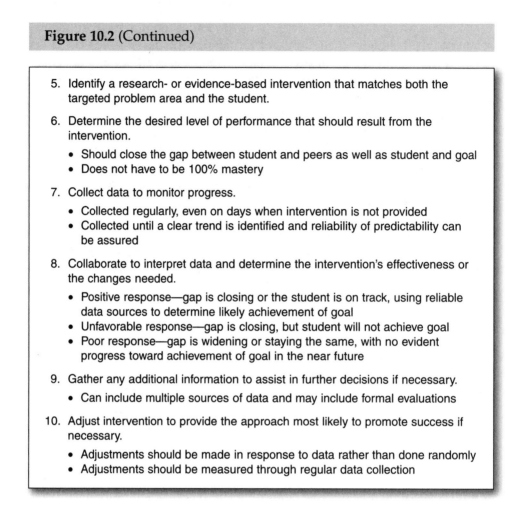

5. Identify a research- or evidence-based intervention that matches both the targeted problem area and the student.

6. Determine the desired level of performance that should result from the intervention.
   • Should close the gap between student and peers as well as student and goal
   • Does not have to be 100% mastery

7. Collect data to monitor progress.
   • Collected regularly, even on days when intervention is not provided
   • Collected until a clear trend is identified and reliability of predictability can be assured

8. Collaborate to interpret data and determine the intervention's effectiveness or the changes needed.
   • Positive response—gap is closing or the student is on track, using reliable data sources to determine likely achievement of goal
   • Unfavorable response—gap is closing, but student will not achieve goal
   • Poor response—gap is widening or staying the same, with no evident progress toward achievement of goal in the near future

9. Gather any additional information to assist in further decisions if necessary.
   • Can include multiple sources of data and may include formal evaluations

10. Adjust intervention to provide the approach most likely to promote success if necessary.
    • Adjustments should be made in response to data rather than done randomly
    • Adjustments should be measured through regular data collection

ADDITIONAL QUESTIONS TO ANSWER IN PROBLEM SOLVING

In any tier, problem solving begins with sharing data and asking questions. These questions are designed to target the specific problem that is occurring and preventing a student from making progress. The questions are *not* designed to challenge the teacher, parent, or school. They are intended to accurately define and validate the problem, which must occur before trying to address the situation. The questions identify the variables inside and outside of the immediate learning setting that may be contributing to the problem. These questions generally fall into three categories: curriculum and instruction, the student as a learner, and the environment. Some of these questions may be asked in a problem-solving team meeting (see Figure 10.3).

Figure 10.3   Possible Questions Asked at a Problem-Solving
Team Meeting

Curriculum and Instruction

- What curriculum is being implemented?
- What research stands behind the curriculum itself?
- What instructional strategies are most commonly implemented?
- Are those strategies research based?
- Does the research match the learners receiving the instruction?
- How are expectations determined?
- How is a student's prior experience assessed, and what response is generated?
- How are foundational skills assessed, reviewed, or built?
- How is relevant vocabulary addressed?
- What is the primary physical format of instruction: whole group, small group, or independent?
- When small-group instruction is used, how are the groups determined?
- What formative assessments are used?
- How are the results from the formative assessments responded to?
- What visual supports are in place in the classroom to assist learners?
- What accommodations are implemented for struggling learners?
- What real-life connections are made in the instruction?

The Student as a Learner

- What academic supports does the student have outside the school setting?
- What challenges does the student face relative to social acceptance?
- What resources are and are not accessible to the student (e.g., time, money, a supportive adult, faith, health, role models, friends, popularity)?
- What motivates this student?
- What experiences has this student had with repeated failure in the same area?
- How strong is the student's desire to achieve academically?
- What are the student's values and goals for the future?
- Who is involved in supporting this student in efforts for success?
- What time of day or day of the week does the student show any positive behavior or achievement?
- Which school employee does this student gravitate to?
- How strongly do social peers influence this student?

The Environment

- Is the instruction provided in a place that limits distractions?
- Are influential peers also receiving the same instruction or intervention?
- Is the instruction or intervention provided by a person who has a healthy relationship with the student?
- Is enough time provided for the intervention to be implemented as designed?
- Are the appropriate resources and materials in good working quality, and are they easily accessible?
- Is the intervention provided in such a way that limits social stigmas?
- Are incentives or motivational aspects built in?

SUMMARY

In all cases, the problem-solving team's role is to use data to assist in decision making about instruction and interventions. The problem-solving teams function differently at different tiers. At Tier 1 a team with a particular teacher may involve assisting that teacher in creating strategies for differentiating instruction. In Tier 2 the team looks at data to create a big picture of conditions, which may be overall strengths and areas of need for a school or grade level. At this level, the team is more focused on the data of small groups of students and individuals. Tier 2 uses data to examine student performance and the effectiveness of an intervention. The problem-solving team assists with both interpretation of data and formulation of an intervention plan. At Tier 3 the team is as individualized as the student needs that are addressed. Again, the team evaluates data for a student's response and determines whether more information from other assessments or evaluations may prove helpful in creating an effective intervention plan. At each level, the problem-solving team functions to assist educators in using data to create plans and solve problems.

QUESTIONS TO CONSIDER

- Do different levels of problem-solving teams exist?
- How do problem-solving teams differ in response to the different needs at each tier?
- How is membership of a problem-solving team determined?
- When is time provided for the problem-solving team to meet?
- What meeting format is used to create efficient meetings?
- How are parents made to feel valued in the problem-solving team meeting?
- What expertise does each person offer to the problem-solving team? Has this been defined or just assumed?
- How often does a Tier 1 problem-solving team meet?
- How often does a Tier 2 problem-solving team meet?
- How often does a Tier 3 problem-solving team meet?
- What structures are in place to ensure efficient and accurate data collection?
- What structures enable educators to communicate concerns?
- What structures enable the problem-solving team to create a non-threatening atmosphere for all people involved?
- What attempts are made to involve students in the problem-solving process?

Resources

PRINCIPLES OF RESPONSE TO INTERVENTION/INSTRUCTION

- All students are included in the RTI framework.
- All students are every person's responsibility.
- Collaboration is essential for success.
- Student needs are met as soon as they are recognized, not only after receiving a label from a special program.
- Progress monitoring guides decisions about curriculum and instruction for a student and for groups of students.
- The rate of progress is as important as the amount of progress made.
- Some students will need supports and services beyond the core curriculum.
- Behavior and academic performances are interrelated.
- Expectations must be clear for students to be successful.
- Student performance is measured in relation to the clearly stated expectations.
- A teacher must recognize and acknowledge when something is not working.
- Data drives decision making.
- Multiple sources of data provide the most detailed picture of a student.
- Tiers of RTI indicate levels of supports, not types of students.
- Tiers are aligned so that a more intensive service supports success at a less intensive level.
- Remediation and intervention are aligned to the core curriculum.
- Quality core instruction in Tier 1 is the foundation for RTI.
- When a group of students all struggle to experience success, instruction must be examined.
- Flexible grouping is one way to provide reteaching and remediation in the classroom.
- Supports exist outside the school setting, and collaboration with the families and agencies providing these supports is essential.

THE PROCESS OF DIFFERENTIATED INSTRUCTION

Step 1: Examine standards and objectives to be taught. Determine the type of knowledge demanded of the standard and/or objective.

Step 2: Establish the conceptual understanding related to the facts and skills required.

Step 3: For any fact or skill, determine the level of fluency needed for mastery.

Step 4: Design independent student activities that incorporate the facts and skills to be addressed along with accommodations for students who need support in achieving mastery of the facts and skills.

Step 5: Reflect on personal knowledge and attitudes related to resources, the content, and the students.

Step 6: Pre-assess students in the areas of knowledge of facts, skills, conceptual understandings, experiences, attitudes, motivations, and ideas.

Step 7: Determine strategies for instruction at different levels of cognitive processing to include concrete, representational, and abstract processes.

Step 8: Determine the flow of classroom activities to include individual, small-group, and whole-group instruction.

Step 9: Determine benchmarks of student performance, and develop tools for ongoing measurement of progress.

Step 10: Develop selections and criteria for the summative product or performance that accurately reflects the intended outcomes of the unit.

CRITICAL DATA PROCESSING QUESTIONS FOR TIER 1 PROBLEM SOLVING FOR GROUPS

Standard, topic, skill, or concept being examined:

What is the expectation or goal for this standard, topic, skill, or concept?

Define the scope of the problem:

1. How many or what percentage of the students across the classroom are considered to be performing below expectations or standards?

2. How many or what percentage of the students across the grade level are considered to be performing below expectations or standards?

3. How many or what percentage of the students across the school are considered to be performing below expectations or standards?

4. How many or what percentage of the students across the district are considered to be performing below expectations or standards?

At what level is there a problem?

Class   Grade   School   District

Analyze the problem:

What is currently being done consistently at the level in which there is a problem?

Assessment tool(s) used to measure achievement	
Assessment tool(s) used to measure progress	
Curriculum	
Instructional practices	
Programs implemented	

Prerequisite skills or concepts needed	
Amount of time provided	
Motivation or relevance through students' eyes	
Efforts to improve on the part of educators	
Priority given	

Stakeholders	
Change agents involved	

Create a hypothesis:

Why is the problem occurring? Which areas above may be problematic?

What would help the situation?

Develop the instruction/intervention design:

Who will implement the plan?	
What actions will be taken?	
How often will the instruction/intervention be provided?	
For how much time will the instruction/intervention be provided?	
For how much time will the instruction/intervention be provided until the plan is reassessed?	

Create a follow-up plan:

Next meeting date: Time: Invitees:

CRITICAL DATA PROCESSING QUESTIONS FOR TIER 1 PROBLEM SOLVING FOR AN INDIVIDUAL

Standard, topic, skill, or concept being examined:

What is the expectation or goal for this standard, topic, skill, or concept?

Define the scope of the problem:

1. How is the student performing in relation to the expectation or goal?

2. How is the student performing in relation to peers in the district?

3. How is the student performing in relation to peers in the school?

4. How is the student performing in relation to peers in grade level?

5. How is the student performing in relation to peers in the class?

6. Are the data consistent across different measures?

Analyze the problem:

Consider each of the following in relation to the concern.

Assessment tool(s) used to measure achievement	

Assessment tool(s) used to measure progress	
Programs implemented	
Prerequisite skills	
Amount of time provided for practice	
Environmental conditions at school and outside	

Student motivation	
Priority communicated by respected people	
Others who may be able to help	

Create a hypothesis:

Why is the problem occurring? Which areas above may be problematic?

What would help this student?

Develop the instruction/intervention design:

Who will implement the plan?	
What actions will be taken?	
How often will the instruction/intervention be provided?	
For how much time will the instruction/intervention be provided?	
For how much time will the instruction/intervention be provided until the plan is re-assessed?	

Considerations for the Development of an Intervention

- The intervention must be research or evidence based.
- The researched population must match the population of the students being considered for the intervention.
- The intervention must be delivered with integrity and fidelity.
- The person delivering the intervention must have the necessary knowledge and professional development to implement the intervention as stated in the research.
- There must be support provided for the intervention plan by all stakeholders, including student and parent.
- There must be consideration regarding the length of time the intervention will be provided.
- The frequency with which the intervention will occur must be reasonable and match the intervention research recommendations.
- There must be a method for monitoring and reporting progress established before beginning the implementation of the intervention.

GUIDING QUESTIONS FOR TIER 2 PROBLEM SOLVING

Name of student(s): _____

Data to examine	Source of data/ measurement tool	When and for how long was data collected?	Are the data consistent over time and other data sources? Yes or No
What data show student performance in relation to the desired learning objective?			
What data show student performance in relation to peers in the grade?			
What data show student performance in relation to peers in the class?			
Other data:			

Analyze the problem:

Consider each of the following in relation to the concern.

Curriculum implemented	
Differentiated instruction provided	
Prerequisite skills	
Consistencies across content areas	
Environmental conditions within and outside the school	

Student motivation	
Parent input	

Create a hypothesis:

Why is the problem occurring? What do the data show as a specific targeted need or area of support?

Develop the instruction/intervention design:

What research- or evidence-based intervention will be provided?	
What materials, space, or scheduling will need to be provided?	
Who will implement the plan?	
What supports will the person implementing the plan receive? From whom?	
How often will the instruction/intervention be provided?	

How often will progress be monitored? With what tool?	
For how long will the instruction/intervention be provided?	
Where will the intervention be provided?	
For how long will the instruction/intervention be provided until the plan is reassessed?	

CONSIDERATIONS FOR MOVING FROM TIER 2 TO TIER 3 SUPPORTS AND SERVICES

Student Name: _____ Date: _____

Targeted area in Tier 2: _____

Instructional materials used: _____

Instructional strategies used: _____

How often each week (frequency): _____

How long for each intervention session (duration): _____

Supports provided by (person): _____

- Has the student had the opportunity to learn in the core instruction?
- Is the Tier 2 instructional program or material research or evidence based, and has it been implemented with fidelity?
- What evidence reflects that?
- What accommodations or supports have been provided during the intervention session?
- How often have data been collected?
- Has there been any evidence of a positive response (high performance) by the student at any time? *The key here is the individual responses, not necessarily successfully meeting the desired level of achievement.*
- Has there been an indicator of a positive response by peers receiving the same intervention?
- Is the trend reliable for predictability (small area between upper and lower control limits)?
- What differences exist between the student and peers receiving the same intervention?

Considerations	Student	Peers
Background knowledge, prior experiences, foundational skills		
Social or emotional conditions		
Motivation		
Aptitude		
Known disability or processing deficit		

• Do the data seem to reflect an issue with programming or student learning? *Programming issues are often reflected by a flat line on graphed data. Student learning issues are often reflected by inconsistent performance data. For behavioral issues, look at student learning considerations.*

If the program is the focus:	If the student learning is the focus:
Consider:	Consider:
• The same program with more time *Is there evidence or research that says more time can produce more positive results? Is that research or evidence based on a profile similar to that of the student of concern?* • A different program than what is used in Tiers 1 and 2 *What gives a different program more potential to meet the learner's needs? Is there reason to think a different program will provide a better fit?*	• Are there obvious obstacles the student faces such as limited English skills or lack of background knowledge? • What occurred during high points to foster achievement? • What does it take to provide those supports or conditions for more regular achievement? *Is this reasonable within Tier 2 or does it require the greater supports and services of Tier 3?* • Is there more information needed about the student's learning and thinking processes? What questions need to be answered? *What evaluations or assessments can provide that information?*

Supports or services needed:	How often:
Where:	What time during the day:

By whom:

Progress monitoring will be collected through the use of:

Data and information will be reviewed on:

STEPS OF PROBLEM SOLVING

1. Identify the specific targeted problem area.

2. Ensure that the quality core curriculum is being administered with fidelity and differentiated strategies that include accommodations.

3. Identify the gap between learner and desired outcome.

4. Identify the gap between learner and peers.

5. Identify a research- or evidence-based intervention that matches both the targeted problem area and the student.

6. Determine the desired level of performance that should result from the intervention.

7. Collect data to monitor progress.

8. Collaborate to interpret data and determine the intervention's effectiveness or the changes needed.

9. Gather any additional information to assist in further decisions if necessary.

10. Adjust intervention to provide the approach most likely to promote success if necessary.

ADDITIONAL CORWIN RESOURCES ON RTI

Using RTI to Teach Literacy to Diverse Learners, K–8, by Sheila Alber-Morgan, 2010.

RTI for Diverse Learners, by Catherine Collier, 2010.

Response to Intervention in Math, by Paul Riccomini, 2010.

55 Tactics for Implementing RTI in Inclusive Settings, by Pam Campbell, 2009.

Tier 3 of the RTI Model, by Sawyer Hunley, 2009.

How RTI Works in Secondary Schools, by Evelyn Johnson, 2009.

A Comprehensive RTI Model, by Cara Shores, 2009.

RTI Assessment Essentials for Struggling Learners, by John Hoover, 2009.

The One-Stop Guide for Implementing RTI, by Maryln Appelbaum, 2008.

Using RTI for School Improvement, by Cara Shores, 2008.

ADDITIONAL CORWIN RESOURCES ON DIFFERENTIATED INSTRUCTION

Beyond Differentiated Instruction, by Jodi O'Meara, 2010.

Differentiation for Real Classrooms, by Kathleen Kryza, 2009.

Differentiated Instructional Strategies for Reading in the Content Areas, 2nd Edition, by Carolyn Chapman, 2009.

Lesson Design for Differentiated Instruction, Grades 4–9, by Kathy Tuchman Glass, 2009.

Differentiating With Graphic Organizers, by Patti Drapeau, 2008.

Differentiation Through Learning Styles and Memory, 2nd Edition, by Marilee Sprenger, 2008.

Differentiated Instructional Strategies in Practice, 2nd Edition, by Gayle Gregory, 2008.

Differentiated Instructional Strategies for Science, Grades K–8, by Gayle Gregory and Elizabeth Hammerman, 2008.

ADDITIONAL CORWIN RESOURCES ON COLLABORATION

The Practice of Authentic PLCs, by Daniel Venables, 2011.

Collaboration and Co-Teaching, by Andrea Honigsfeld, 2010.

Effective Collaboration for Educating the Whole Child, by Carol Kochhar-Bryant, 2010.

Collaborative Teaching in Secondary Schools, by Wendy Murawski, 2009.

Purposeful Co-Teaching, by Greg Conderman, 2008.

A Guide to Co-Teaching With Paraeducators, by Ann Nevin, 2008.

References

Brown-Chidsey, R., Bronaugh, L., & McGraw, K. (2009). *RTI in the classroom: Guidelines and recipes for success.* New York: Guilford Press.

Burns, M. K., & Coolong-Chaffin, M. (2006). Response to intervention: The role of and effect on school psychology. *School Psychology Forum: Research and Practice, 1*(1), 3–15.

Covey, S. B. (1990). *The 7 habits of highly effective people: Powerful lessons in personal change.* New York: Fireside.

Dawkins, B. (2010). *Intentional teaching: The let me learn classroom in action.* Thousand Oaks, CA: Corwin.

Fisher, D., & Frey, N. (2001). *Responsive curriculum design in secondary schools: Meeting the diverse needs of students.* Lanham, MD: Scarecrow Press.

Gardner, H. (1993). *Frames of mind: The theory of multiple intelligences.* New York: Basic Books.

Gentry, M. L. (1999). *Promoting student achievement and exemplary classroom practices through cluster grouping: A research-based alternative to heterogeneous elementary classrooms (RM99138).* Storrs: University of Connecticut, National Research Center on the Gifted and Talented.

Gregory, G. H., & Kuzmich, L. (2004). *Data driven differentiation in the standards-based classroom.* Thousand Oaks, CA: Corwin.

Gresham, F. M. (2007). The evolution of the RTI concept: Empirical foundations and recent developments. In S. R. Jimerson, M. K. Burns, & A. M. VanDerHeyden (Eds.), *Handbook of response to intervention: The science and practice of assessment and intervention* (pp. 10–24). New York: Springer.

Howard, M. (2009). *RtI from all sides: What every teacher needs to know.* Portsmouth, NH: Heinemann.

Jimerson, S. R., Burns, M. K., & VanDerHeyden, A. M. (Eds.). (2007). *Handbook of response to intervention: The science and practice of assessment and intervention.* New York: Springer.

Leuchovius, D. (2006). *The role of parents in dropout prevention: Strategies that promote graduation and school achievement.* Retrieved January 21, 2011, from http://www.ncset.org/publications/viewdesc.asp?id=3135

Lipson, M., & Wixson, K. (2010). *Successful approaches to RTI collaborative practices for improving K–12 literacy.* Newark, DE: International Reading Association.

Madaus, G. F., & Stufflebeam, D. C. (1989). *Educational evaluation: Classic works of Ralph W. Tyler.* New York: Springer.

Maslow, A. H. (1998). *Toward a psychology of being.* Hoboken, NJ: John Wiley & Sons.

Miller, J., & Desberg, P. (2009). *Understanding and engaging adolescents.* Thousand Oaks, CA: Corwin.

Murawski, W. W. (2005). Addressing diverse needs through co-teaching: Take "baby steps." *Kappa Delta Pi Record, 41*(2), 77–82.

National Association of State Directors of Special Education. (2006). *Response to intervention: Policy considerations and implementation.* Alexandria, VA: Author.

National Center on Response to Intervention. (n.d.-a). *Progress monitoring tools chart.* Retrieved January 18, 2011, from http://www.rti4success.org/tools_charts/progress.php

National Center on Response to Intervention. (n.d.-b). *What is RTI?* Retrieved January 18, 2011, from http://www.rti4success.org/

National Council of Teachers of Mathematics. (2006). *Curriculum focal points for prekindergarten through grade 8 mathematics: A quest for coherence.* Reston, VA: Author.

O'Meara, J. (2010). *Beyond differentiated instruction.* Thousand Oaks, CA: Corwin.

Riccomini, P. J., & Witzel, B. S. (2010). *Response to intervention in math.* Thousand Oaks, CA: Corwin.

Rudebusch, J. (2008). *The source for RtI.* East Moline, IL: LinguiSystems.

Safer, N., & Fleischman, S. (2005). How student progress monitoring improves instruction. *Educational Leadership, 62*(5), 81–83.

Shalaway, L. (2005). *Learning to teach . . . not just for beginners* (3rd ed.). New York: Scholastic.

Simon, K. G. (2002). The blue blood is bad, right? *Educational Leadership, 60*(1), 24–28.

Tomlinson, C. A. (2003). *Fulfilling the promise of the differentiated classroom: Strategies and tools for responsive teaching.* Alexandria, VA: Association for Supervision and Curriculum Development.

Tomlinson, C., Kaplan, S. N., Renzulli, J. S., Purcell, J. H., Leppien, J. H., & Burns, D. E. (2002). *The parallel curriculum: A design to develop high potential and challenge high-ability learners.* Thousand Oaks, CA: Corwin.

Tucker, M. S., & Codding, J. B. (1998). *Standards for our schools: How to set them, measure them, and reach them.* San Francisco: Jossey-Bass.

Wiggins, G., & McTighe, J. (2005). *Understanding by design* (2nd ed.). Alexandria, VA: Association for Supervision and Curriculum Development.

Index

CORWIN

A SAGE Company

The Corwin logo—a raven striding across an open book—represents the union of courage and learning. Corwin is committed to improving education for all learners by publishing books and other professional development resources for those serving the field of PreK–12 education. By providing practical, hands-on materials, Corwin continues to carry out the promise of its motto: **"Helping Educators Do Their Work Better."**